THE FAMILY YEARS: A GUIDE TO POSITIVE PARENTING

Michael Colin Macpherson

Winston Press

to my parents, who gave me a sense of my own worth

Library of Congress Catalog Card Number: 80-53740

ISBN: 0-86683-772-8 (previously ISBN: 0-03-059131-7)

Printed in the United States of America.

Winston Press, Inc.
430 Oak Grove
Minneapolis, Minnesota 55403

5 4 3 2

TABLE OF CONTENTS

INTRODUCTION

This is a book about families. More specifically, it is a book about—and for—families who are experiencing typical family problems.

I am a family therapist. When a family comes to me for treatment, I begin by making certain assumptions about them. These assumptions provide me with a way to approach the family, determine the nature and extent of their problems, and start exploring possible solutions. Since those same assumptions are the basis for this book, I will introduce and explain them here.

1. *A family is a system.* By this I mean that whatever affects one family member almost always affects everyone else in the family. This may not be obvious but it is still true. By extension, problems in a family are felt by everyone. They may seem to be confined to one or two family members, and no one else may appear to be affected, but this is usually an illusion. As soon as someone in a family begins to talk about his or her thoughts or feelings, it becomes clear that everyone is influenced by them to some extent.

2. *Family problems are often due to poor communication.* In even the healthiest families people do not always communicate clearly. They do not tell others what they expect from them. They make assumptions about what others like and dislike, what they want and do not want, and seldom verify their assumptions. These behaviors, which are common to troubled families, interfere with problem-solving. Good communication and a real sharing of feelings are essential to effective problem-solving. The family conference is often the best problem-solving setting, but even it will not work if family members cannot or will not communicate freely with one another.

3. *Everyone in a family sees problems from his or her own point of view.* This can lead to some family members taking

a defensive stance and projecting their feelings and motives onto others. Often the way to change these unhealthy behaviors is by encouraging family members to share their feelings and points of view.

4. *Everyone in a family is a separate person with an identity of his or her own.* This may seem to contradict my first assumption—that a family is a system—but it does not. To say that people affect one another is not the same as saying that they define one another's identities. A mother may feel as if her only identity is that of motherhood, but this is not true. It is very important for every person in a family to see and appreciate his or her own separateness; to know where he or she stops and others begin. Otherwise, problems cannot be solved.

In my years of working with families, certain issues have come up again and again. Much of this book will be concerned with exploring these problem issues, including:

- how to set limits and make rules and what to do if they don't work;
- how to deal with transition times and other changes;
- how to deal with conflicts;
- how to hold family conferences;
- how to deal with the turbulence of adolescence;
- how parents can avoid living their lives through their children;
- how parents can take care of themselves; and
- how parents can improve their relationship with each other.

As I mentioned earlier, this book is about families. But since it focuses on (although it is not limited to) the relationships between parents and children, it is also a parenting book. From my perspective, successful parenting is a combination of three elements: (1) good parenting techniques; (2) an awareness of how the family works together as a system and how each member fits into that system; and (3) an awareness of one's own personality and how it affects the family as a whole.

When I talk about techniques, I am referring to applied psychology plus some common sense (or maybe it's the other way around!). Certain techniques can greatly improve one's parenting skills. In this book I will present some of the techniques which my years of working with families have shown to be the most useful. But I also want to go beyond mere techniques and into areas not explored by most parenting books, including an awareness of how the family works together as a system and how an awareness of one's own personality can affect that system.

Why am I so concerned with self-awareness? Because no matter how well someone learns or applies specific techniques, they are often of limited use. Many family problems—especially parent-child conflicts—cannot be solved by techniques alone. It usually takes an added awareness of the roles each member plays before a difficulty can really be resolved. So I will frequently ask you to look inside yourself, to be aware of the kind of person you are, and to explore your expectations and those you make about the other members of your family. I will also ask you to reclaim parts of yourself—parts which you may have forgotten about but which still shape you as a person and as a parent.

Self-awareness is important for yet another reason. Often, when parents are truly aware of themselves, they find that the correct techniques for solving their family problems emerge naturally. And, in the final analysis, that is the true goal of this book: helping families to help themselves.

I. PARENTING TECHNIQUES AND THE IMPORTANCE OF SELF-AWARENESS

SCHOOL PHOBIA: A CASE STUDY

Linda's daughter Tammy was in the first grade. The school was a nice one, and both Linda and Tammy liked the first-grade teacher.

But Tammy was having problems. She dawdled in the morning and she was reluctant to leave the car when Linda drove her to school.

The most distressing problem, though, was more complicated. Soon after the school year began, Tammy started having bad dreams. The theme was always the same: something scary was going to happen to her at school. Since Linda was a good mother, she was concerned about her daughter. She had read a few parenting books and had learned some of the techniques necessary for dealing with fears of this kind. She knew, for instance, that it was important to let her daughter talk about her dreams and avoid trying to explain or interpret them until Tammy had had the chance to do so herself. She also knew not to give too much support or comfort right away.

This latter technique was hard for Linda to implement, however. Often she found herself consoling Tammy almost immediately. She couldn't help it. Besides, it didn't seem to be doing any harm.

Linda spent several hours over the next two months trying to help Tammy with her nightmares, but nothing she did seemed to work. Convinced that her techniques were wrong, Linda did more reading. But she came away confused and frustrated because she was already doing what the books said to do—most of the time. Finally, it was Tammy herself who supplied the answer.

Tammy woke one night from a bad dream and asked if she could come into her mother's bed. Linda agreed. When they were comfortable, Linda asked Tammy to tell her about her dream. After Tammy had talked for a while, she suddenly stopped and pointed to her mother's hands and asked her why they were shaking. Linda hadn't even realized that her hands were shaking—but they were.

Linda puzzled over this the next day. Then she remembered something she had pushed out of her conscious memory. She remembered how scared *she* had been as a child entering the first grade, and she also remembered that she had had bad dreams at the time. She realized that part of her was still a little girl who was scared of school—and that *her daughter's fears were scaring her!* Then she understood why she felt slightly tense and nervous whenever Tammy related one of her nightmares. They were touching off her own unresolved fears.

Over the next few weeks, Linda dealt with her old childhood fears. The next time Tammy had a bad dream and wanted to talk about it, Linda felt very calm and not at all nervous or afraid. Nor did she feel the need to interrupt or to console Tammy right away, as she had done in the past.

Tammy responded by opening up to her mother even more. Soon she was able to articulate her biggest fear: that her mother would leave her at school one day and never return to pick her up. Linda listened patiently. Then together they talked calmly and quietly about Tammy's dreams and what they meant.

The next few weeks saw a marked decrease in Tammy's nightmares. Each succeeding dream became less frightening, and finally they stopped altogether.

COMMENTS ON THE CASE STUDY

Although Linda knew the correct techniques for dealing with her daughter's problem as soon as it arose, she stopped herself from fully using them at first. Intellectually she knew what to do to help Tammy, but emotionally she wasn't quite ready to use her knowledge. Her own insecurities were getting in the way.

Tammy's fears were scaring Linda. She showed this by being tense and nervous and by interrupting her daughter while she was talking. And Linda's fears adversely affected Tammy. Tammy *knew* that her mother was afraid, and this in turn increased her own fear level. It also stopped her from fully expressing what was frightening her. In a subtle yet very real way Linda was giving her daughter the message that *it was not okay to express her fears.*

As soon as Linda became aware of herself and her own fears, she began to deal with them effectively. She could then make proper use of the techniques she already knew to help her daughter. And she could do so without sending conflicting messages. Before she achieved self-awareness, Linda had been *telling* her daughter that it was okay to talk about her fears while *showing* her (by her shaking hands) that it was definitely not okay. Once she was able to quiet her own fears, Linda felt comfortable listening to Tammy, responding to her, and comforting her at the appropriate times. And as Tammy shared her dreams with her mother, explored what was causing them, and began to feel more secure, she was better able to deal with her problem on her own.

****

What does this mean for you as a parent? It's no secret that the right techniques and a certain degree of self-awareness can be useful. But it takes time to learn techniques, and it also takes time to achieve self-awareness.

If you are an average parent, you probably want some immediate answers. Perhaps as you read this you can hear your kids fighting again and you want to know what to do *right now* before you decide to flush them down the toilet!

All I can say is: Relax and have faith. There *are* answers—I hope you will find some in this book—but they are neither quick nor easy.

Whenever I have a problem in my own life, I'm often impatient with how much time and energy it takes to work through it. I want it to just go away, especially if it's particularly painful. But it never works like that (or almost never), and when I'm honest with myself I usually realize that I've had the problem for a long time and it won't go away unless I work patiently at resolving it.

The same is true for you, too. It's natural to be impatient and to want quick answers. But do try to be kind to yourself. Give yourself enough time and space to explore any parenting problems you may have before you set about trying to resolve them.

It may help to start by thinking of something you enjoy doing. Maybe it's cooking or painting pictures or working on your car. How do you approach *these* tasks? More often than not, you probably take your time and make careful plans. You want to do the best you can. And when you meet an obstacle or become frustrated, you probably avoid rushing through things. You want to do the best job you can on any task you undertake.

You need to adopt the same attitude when you approach the tasks of parenting. If anything, you need to be even more patient and more dedicated, because people are not as easy to deal with as cakes or cars!

Let's begin exercising your patience and dedication now. I would like you to get a pencil and a piece of paper and write down your responses to some questions about yourself. You don't have to write long, involved answers; a couple of sentences or key words will do. When you have finished, put the paper away. Later in the book I'll show you how you can use this information.

I chose the following particular questions because in my years of working with families they have proved to be useful tools. They can often stimulate the self-awareness necessary to solve some parenting difficulties.

- What did it *feel* like to be a member of your family?
- What were you like as a child?
- What would you have been like as a child if you could have been different?
- What were you like as a teenager?
- What would you have been like as a teenager if you could have been different?
- If you could change one thing about the way you are now, what would it be?
- What scared you the most when you were young?
- Is there something you would like to do now that you never had the chance to do before? If so, what?
- Is there someone you know whom you would like to model yourself after—or even be? If so, whom?
- What do you see your children doing when they become adults? Or, in other words, what kinds of lives do you think they will have?

The following questions explore your thoughts and feelings about your partner. In this context, "partner" refers to the other parent of your child or children. Please answer these questions even if you are not currently living with this person.

- What was your first impression of your partner?
- What is the thing you like most about him or her?
- What is the thing you like least about him or her?
- What is one thing you would like to say to your partner that you have never said?
- If there was a safe way of doing so, would you say this unspoken thing to him or her? If not, what would stop you?

Now put your answers away in a safe place and just forget about them for a while. We'll come back to them later.

II. SETTING LIMITS AND MAKING RULES

Rules come in many shapes and sizes. Some are handed down in the form of laws by the government. Still others originate with our churches or peer groups. There are externally-imposed rules that dictate how we should act toward one another and internally-imposed rules that structure our personal conduct and moral codes. Regardless of their source, though, all rules have something in common: *they are intended to guide our behavior.*

Rules range from strict principles to local customs. In the case of a strict principle, specific people or groups are usually responsible for setting the rule, defining it in explicit terms, and enforcing it. In the case of a local custom, there is usually no identifiable source of the rule, but people follow it anyway. When asked why they do a certain thing in a certain way, they're likely to say, "Because that's the way it's always been done!"

Families make rules to guide the behavior of their members. Some of those rules carry the same weight as strict principles—especially those which are made by parents for their children. But many others are not openly stated and are more like customs.

In many families these "customary" kinds of rules concern matters such as how and when family members are supposed to show affection, when it is okay to get angry, and who can get angry at whom. When these kinds of rules are broken, it is difficult to predict what the aftereffects will be. Often family members will only be able to say that they feel uneasy because someone isn't acting the way he or she "should."

Although "customary" rules are interesting and worthy of attention, I will not discuss them here. Instead, I will focus on rules which are made by parents to guide their children's behavior—the kinds of rules *you* make. And I will begin by discussing techniques you can combine with your own self-awareness to get a good start on this important task.

In order to be a successful rule-maker, you first have to decide exactly what you want to accomplish with rules. And since rules are basically ways to get your children to do what you want them to do—or to stop them from doing what you *don't* want them to do—you first have to know what you do and do not want them to do. These first steps are crucial. The next step is to communicate these things to your children in a clear and intelligible way.

The best way to begin this process is by sitting down and doing some serious thinking. You may find it useful to jot down a few notes along the way.

Since rules cover so many different kinds of behavior, you might also find it helpful to categorize the ones you come up with. Try using the following four categories. There may be some overlap, but most of the time it should be fairly clear which rule belongs where.

I.   *Rules that organize and structure your family.*
     Examples: when everyone is expected to come to dinner; times when your children may have friends over to visit.
II. *Rules concerning health and safety.*
     Example: a prohibition against playing with matches or medicine.
III. *Rules that guide your children's personal development.*
     Examples: school attendance and homework; bedtimes; dating.
IV. *Rules that facilitate your own well-being.*
     Examples: respect for your privacy; the division of household chores.

Under each category write down what you want to accomplish with the rules you list there. A good strategy is to start off with a *general* idea and then, little by little, make it more specific.

For example, one of the things you may want to accomplish with rules that fall into the third category is to have your children do well in school. That's the general idea. Now, how can you put this into practice so that they know specifically what is expected of them? Working from the general to the specific, you might come up with a set of rules like this:

1. They have to attend school.
2. They have to do their homework.
3. More specifically, they have to do their homework every day.
4. Even more specifically, they have to do their homework before dinner.

It is easier to be specific with some rules than with others. Parents usually have more difficulty with the third and fourth categories than with the first two. The reasons for this might be worth talking about.

Rules about organization and structure usually do not pose problems as long as you can be clear and consistent about them. Health and safety rules are also fairly easy. Common sense determines many of these, and there is also a whole set of agreed-upon social norms, or societal guidelines, available to help you with them. For instance, almost everyone agrees that young children should not play in the street.

Rules for children's personal development are not as clear-cut, however. Although there *are* some societal guidelines, they tend to get fuzzy very quickly, which means that *you* must be the final authority. This situation can make parents unsure of themselves. For example, there are not generally accepted guidelines governing dating, at least not to my knowledge. Middle-class parents have the vague feeling that children shouldn't rush into serious dating before they are old enough to handle it. But this leaves a great deal of room for interpretation. How old do children have to be before they can go steady? Or have sexual experiences? There are really no easy answers to questions like these. You are on your own here, and you are an exceptional parent if this doesn't make you feel unsure and defensive. To make matters worse, a child will invariably push and test a parent who is unsure about a rule to find out where the limit actually is, and this can lead to arguments and conflicts.

There is no real answer to this dilemma. Your children will almost certainly challenge these kinds of rules. The best strategy to use when you are making them is simply to take your time and make sure you really believe in them yourself. You may need to do some serious thinking, especially about such sensitive issues as sex. It may also help to talk with other parents.

The fourth category—rules that facilitate your own well-being—also causes problems for parents. There are few well-established guidelines to help you in this area, and there are often social forces working *against* you, too. I'll discuss these issues in more detail later.

So far it may sound as if all you have to do to be a successful rule-maker is to sit down, figure out what rules you want to make, and then—presto!—your family will run smoothly from that point on. But of course this isn't true. There are many limiting factors, and often you will have to compromise or modify what you want in light of what is possible in your family and/or what you are comfortable with. One such limiting factor is the need to be consistent about the rules you make.

Consistency is one of those words that is used a lot in parenting books and classes. To avoid any possible confusion, I'll define what I mean when I use it here: Being consistent means that the behavior you do or do not allow according to any *one* rule will be the same from day to day. Being consistent is not always easy, but the effort is well worth it.

Parents often have trouble understanding *why* consistency is important. As a result, they have problems being consistent. I'll give you an example in case this is sounding a bit confusing to you.

Imagine that you have a job and your boss is vague about the time you need to be there in the morning. He says that everyone has to arrive sometime between 8:00 A.M. and 10:00 A.M. After several months he decides that not enough work is being done (everyone is getting there exactly at 10:00), so he says that everyone must arrive by 8:00. You grumble, but you go along with the new rule. A few days later, feeling that he is being too strict, your boss returns to his original 8:00 to 10:00 idea. Now what do you do?

Your boss doesn't seem to know what he wants you to do, and this makes it harder for you to make a decision. You'd like to get there at 10:00 (you thought that was the best idea he ever had), but he doesn't seem to like that idea even though he *says* he does. What if he changes his mind again on the day you decide to be brave and arrive at 10:00? You will probably feel confused and apprehensive because of his inconsistency, and it may even make you mad.

This is how inconsistent rules look to children. We all—both children *and* adults—want to know what is expected of us by those people who have some control over our lives. Specifically, we want to know that what is permitted today will also be permitted tomorrow. In other words, you need to be consistent within *each* particular rule that governs your children's behavior. This is not the same as saying that you must make the same rules for every situation, however.

For example, let's say that you feel strongly that your children need to be in bed by 8:00 P.M. That's the rule, and you are strict about it. But when it comes to dinnertime you don't feel the need to put your children (or you) on such a strict schedule, so the rule is that "around five" everyone should start getting ready to eat. Although in one case you are holding to a strict schedule and in another you are not, you are *not* being inconsistent because dinnertime and bedtime are two *different* situations. Don't worry that your children will get confused; children handle differences like this quite well.

Consistency and clearness usually go hand in hand. It is generally much easier to make consistent rules if you have thought them out ahead of time—that is, if you are clear about them. Another important factor to consider— and one that relates to the two I have just mentioned—is acceptability. The rules you make should be ones that you yourself can accept and live with, or you will probably find that you apply them inconsistently.

Health and safety rules are usually pretty easy to live with. For instance, it's reasonable to decide that a two-year-old is *never* to go into the street by himself or herself or that a five-year-old is *never* to turn on the gas unless an adult is there to supervise. There should be *no* exceptions to these rules, which means that a parent can be consistent in their application.

Some personal development rules can also be clear-cut. For example, you may feel strongly that you want your children to be able to express their anger and frustration without violence. Your rule in this case might be that they are *never* to hit one another. If you decide ahead of time that you will tolerate no exceptions, you can be clear and consistent about this rule.

But now consider another rule that also falls into the personal development category. Let's say that your bedtime rule states that your children must be in their rooms by 8:00 P.M. but they can play or watch television until 9:00. The only trouble is that sometimes their play gets too loud, and you find yourself putting them to bed a little early. Because you are being inconsistent by making them go to bed before 9:00, you can expect some trouble.

A better way to handle this would be to change the rule. The new rule might state that your children must be in their rooms by 8:00 and that they can read or watch television until 9:00 but they cannot play. You can live with this new rule since it takes care of the noise problem that bothered you before. And because you can live with it and you are comfortable with it, you can also be consistent.

You may want to experiment with a number of different rules to discover which ones will work for you and your family. This may cause some confusion in the beginning, but it will not do any damage and will help you to be clear about the rules you want to make.

For example, imagine that it's the end of summer vacation and time to get back to a school bedtime schedule. Since your children are a year older now, you decide to let them stay up later than you allowed them to last year. You aren't sure about how much later, though, so you want to experiment with some different times. Tell your children that you *are* experimenting, by the way; children usually get into the spirit of the experiment. Just make sure that the final decision is *your* decision. Do *not* let the outcome rest only on their performance. I'll explain why this is so important.

Let's say that you tell your children something like this: "You can stay up half an hour later on school nights as long as you aren't too sleepy to get up and go to school in the morning." This may work for a while—most children love challenges—but in the end you will wish you had never thought of it. What if your children *are* sleepy in the morning? How sleepy is too sleepy, and who will determine this? What if they get themselves up and even get off to school on time but are grumpy all day because they haven't gotten enough sleep? Then what will you do? Setting up the situation in this way leaves the final outcome up to them; at least that's the way they will see it. And you'll end up having to argue with them.

A better way to proceed is to say something like this: "You are a year older now, and I think you can start staying up later on school nights. Let's try half an hour and see how it goes. But *I* will be the one who decides whether or not it works." This won't leave any doubt as to who has the final say!

So far I've discussed three elements in successful rule-making:

1. Know what you want your children to do.
2. Be consistent.
3. Make rules that you yourself can live with.

A fourth element is just as important, and I want to deal with that now:

4. *Tell* your children what your rules are.

There is nothing mysterious or particularly difficult about this, but many parents have trouble with it. Somehow they never get around to verbalizing rules to their children in clear, precise language—and their children never quite know what is expected of them.

For instance, let's say that your five-year-old has gotten into the habit of pulling the dog's tail. You don't want her to do this, so you frown at her every time you catch her at it. This is not enough. It's better to be explicit in stating what is and is not allowed. "I want you to stop pulling the dog's tail" is far more effective than a dirty look.

You don't need to go into elaborate detail about why you don't want her to pull the dog's tail, though, and this leads to the next rule-making element:

5. Keep your rules as simple as possible.

This is especially important for children under five, although all children appreciate it. Always try to use as few words as you can to convey what you want. For example:

To a four-year-old: "I do not want you to EVER play in the street."

To a ten-year-old: "I want you in bed by 9:00 on school nights. On weekends you can stay up until 10:30."

If you make a rule and find that it gets too complicated, or has too many exceptions, it may be because you are trying to squeeze too much into that one rule. Try separating it into two or more rules. You may even discover that a particular situation does not lend itself to restrictions. In that case it might be best to give up and not have a rule about it at all. True, your children (and you) may be a bit confused as a result, but this is still preferable to living with unworkable rules that almost always lead to conflict.

What about exceptions? Every rule (except for health and safety rules) will have exceptions once in a while. The best approach to this is to define exceptions as such and state clearly that the rules themselves haven't changed.

In many of the above examples, I have used what psychologists call "I-messages" in phrasing the rules. "I-messages" are statements made in the first person—"I want you to do this," "I do not want you to do that," and so on. Some psychologists suggest not using I-messages. In their opinion, the bedtime rule would be better stated like this:

To a ten-year-old: "The rule in this house is that you are to be in bed by 9:00 on school nights. The rule on weekends is that you can stay up until 10:30."

While I don't believe that this is a critical issue, I do feel that the first person approach has some advantages. It's more direct and more honest. After all, you *are* the one who is making the rules and enforcing them. You know this, and your children know it too. So why pretend that the rules originate somewhere else?

The assumption underlying the second approach—the one without I-messages—is that the more impersonal phrasing lessens the chance that rule time will result in a confrontation between you and your children, a battle of *you* against *them*. But rule time is almost always a head-on encounter anyway; by not using I-messages you are only trying to avoid acknowledging this.

Many parents wonder whether children should have a voice in determining the rules that govern their behavior—and if so, how much. I believe that children *should* have some say in this matter. As they become older and more responsible, they should play a more active role in setting up the rules and limits that affect them. Maturity is the issue here, not age. Although maturity usually comes with increasing age, this is not always true, and you need to keep this in mind as you consider your own children.

Letting children take some control works best if you first determine limits and then let your children make some choices within these limits. This can be a source of conflict, of course, especially if you have children of differing ages. For if you allow your older children to take more control over the rules, your younger children may feel you're being unfair. If this happens, you may want to say something like this:

> To your younger child: "I know you feel it isn't fair that Jane (the older child) can do some things you can't do. But she's older now, and the rules are different for older children."

Younger children can deal with age-related privileges if you present them in this way. The implication (which you can state if you want) is that they will also have such privileges when they get older. Whatever you do, though, avoid saying something like, "You can't do what Jane does because you're too young." Putting it this way hurts the younger child and makes it seem as if there is something inherently wrong with being young.

In general, I believe that rule-making works best when it's a family affair. This means holding a family conference in which everyone has the chance to both talk and be listened to. A major advantage to this approach is that everyone gets the opportunity to learn *all* the rules—not just the ones that affect them.

If your family is like most, you probably haven't tried this yet. And you probably already have a set of rules. Even so, it's still a good idea to hold a conference. You may find that not everyone knows all of the rules or that some rules need to be changed or modified.

You may also find that your children are dissatisfied with some new or existing rules. It's very important to let them express their thoughts and feelings. This means being patient and listening to what they have to say. You don't have to agree with everything they say, but you should listen. Children who feel they have really been heard tend to have far fewer complaints in the long run.

A family conference is also a good time for you to explain why you feel a particular rule is necessary. Be honest and straightforward about your reasons. You may discover that some of them aren't as valid as you thought!

Once you have your family's rules worked out (it will probably take more than one conference), it's a good idea to write them down. This is especially useful for young children. Feel free to be creative. Use crayons or brightly-colored paints and list the rules on a sheet of butcher paper. Or, for very young children, you might want to use a combination of pictures and words. Try to get everyone involved in this activity.

Successful rule-making depends on the principles we've been discussing. Here's a brief summary: Rules are ways to guide children's behavior. In order to make good rules, you must first know what you want to accomplish. You need to be consistent. You may need to experiment. Within the limits you set, your children will benefit from having some say in determining the rules. And rule-making works best when it's a family affair.

Now let's look at how one family dealt with these issues.

THE TV BLUES: A CASE STUDY

The Morrisons' nine-year-old twins, Belynda and Kevin, loved to watch television. But Jan Morrison was worried about how much television her children were watching; some days it seemed like that's all they did.

After Jan and her husband Mike talked it over, they decided that it was time to set some rules. As things stood now, there were no rules and the twins were allowed to watch as much as they wanted until it was time for bed. Occasionally Jan or Mike would censor a program they felt was unsuitable for nine-year-olds, but this was the extent of the limits they imposed.

One night the family got together after dinner to discuss the television issue. Mike announced that from now on there would be a limit as to how much the twins could watch. They could continue to choose the programs they wanted to see, but they could watch television for only two hours a day.

Belynda suggested that they be allowed to save up time since they watched less than two hours on some days. The parents agreed, although they set an absolute limit of three hours a day.

Although Jan had anticipated arguments when it came time to turn the television off, she was pleasantly surprised to find that her children adjusted to the new situation rather well. There were *some* arguments, of course, but they didn't last long. The real problems began about a month later.

Mike worked in a shop where the noise level was very high, and he looked forward every day to coming home to some peace and quiet. But he usually found his children watching television at that time. Although it bothered him, he didn't say anything, feeling that it would be unfair of him to change the rules now that they were all worked out.

What he *did* do was ask them to keep the television volume turned down low after he got home. Sometimes they remembered and sometimes they didn't, and sometimes what *they* considered low wasn't what Mike considered low. They had some arguments about this, and for a while Jan and Mike considered moving the television into the family room, although nothing was done about this.

Finally Mike came home one evening after a particularly difficult day to find the television at full blast—and he blew up. He yelled at the twins to turn the television off and added that since they hadn't followed the rule about keeping it low, there would be no more television for the rest of the week.

A couple of days later the family sat down together again to talk about the situation.

Kevin and Belynda complained that their parents had broken their word. First they had said that the twins could watch whatever they wanted for two hours a day and now they couldn't watch at all! That wasn't fair!

Mike agreed that Kevin and Belynda had a right to feel as they did. Then he explained how *he* felt and how important it was to him to have some quiet after he got home from work.

After everyone finished talking, Jan suggested that they make one small change in the rules. From now on the television would be off from the time Mike got home until after dinner.

Everyone agreed. And that was the end of the Morrisons' television conflict.

COMMENTS ON THE CASE STUDY

From the beginning, the Morrisons approached their problem constructively. They knew what they wanted to accomplish, and they introduced rules to see that this happened. They talked about the situation as a family, and the parents were careful to listen to their children's opinions and objections. And, although Mike and Jan set the final limits (the number of hours that could be watched per day), the twins could make some choices within these limits.

So why didn't the first rule they came up with work? Because the parents—and Mike in particular—weren't really comfortable with it and were not able to be consistent about enforcing it. The source of the inconsistency was in the free-choice aspect of the arrangement. It was implied that within the limits set by the parents the twins could do as they pleased. There were no rules about noise level, just as there were none about which programs the children could watch. In reality, though, there were different rules for different time periods. The rules depended on Mike's tolerance for noise on any particular day.

Although this conflict was finally resolved, it might have been settled more quickly if this situation had been approached as an experiment. This tactic is especially useful whenever parents need to make rules about behavior that has not been governed in the past. It is difficult to introduce rules into new situations and have them work immediately without any hitches.

III. WHAT TO DO WHEN THE RULES DON'T WORK

The art of good rule-making involves far more than techniques alone. No matter how careful, consistent, and clear you are, there are bound to be times when the rules and limits you set simply don't work the way you want them to. What happens next often depends on the kind of person you are and how this influences the rules you make, how well you ask for things for yourself, and how you handle confrontation. Once again, I'm talking about the importance of self-awareness.

Whenever you make rules, you bring your own personal style to the task. Rule-making is *not* just a mechanical process. True, there are techniques you can learn—how to phrase rules, what to say if your child objects, how to be consistent, and so forth—but you will always learn them (and implement them) in your *own* way. And your own shortcomings and deficiencies may show up here. Of course, your positive attributes will, too, but since this chapter focuses on those instances when rules don't work, I want you to be willing to forget about those for a while and concentrate on your shortcomings. This may not be pleasant, but it will be helpful in the long run.

As a general rule, whatever facets of your personality give you problems in other areas of your life will also give you problems when you make rules. For example, do you have a short temper? If so, you may find yourself getting angry too quickly if your children do not follow the rules. Are you too much of a perfectionist? If you are, you may expect your children to do exactly as you say and follow every rule to the letter, and you may be irritated or upset if they don't. Are you the kind of person who will do anything to avoid an argument? Then you may have trouble being firm when it comes to rules, or you may find yourself making exceptions in order to avoid conflict or arguments. Do you have a hard time standing up for yourself and telling others what you want from them? Then you may have difficulties with the rules that affect your own well-being.

In my experience working with families, the last two personality characteristics—the desire to avoid arguments, and the lack of ability to stand up for oneself—are the ones that cause the most problems. Let's begin by looking at these more closely, starting with the last one first.

The final category in Chapter Two dealt with rules created more for your *own* well-being. For instance, you may want some quiet time when you come home from work, so you make a rule to see that you get it. When you make a rule like this you are saying, *"I want something for myself."* There is nothing wrong with this. You ask for things for yourself from other adults, and you should also feel it's okay to ask for things from your children.

If you have trouble with these kinds of rules, it may well be that you don't feel you deserve the things you're asking for. Children sense this lack of self-confidence. They learn that when Mom or Dad makes a certain kind of rule it doesn't have real meaning, and they push against it to see how far they can go. For example, let's say that you claim to want half an hour to yourself after you come home from work. If you don't mean it—if you feel somehow as if you don't deserve this quiet time alone—your children probably won't let you have it. They realize that if they're persistent enough you'll give in. When children push like this, they aren't being mean. Rather, they are trying to find out where the limits actually are; they want to know what is *really* going to be allowed and what isn't.

If you have ever experienced this with your children, you know how exasperating it can be. The children seem to totally ignore your requests for some time and space for yourself. It seems as if they are always "at" you and can never leave you alone. You may even feel that they're deliberately taking advantage of you.

What can you do? Start by re-directing your energies away from trying to make the rules work and into *yourself*. This isn't a problem that can be solved by better techniques or better rules; as long as you feel, deep inside, that you don't deserve things for yourself, it won't do any good to ask your children to honor your requests. You need to develop a sense of yourself as a person who is entitled to the things you ask for. This can be especially difficult for women who were brought up to be caregivers, to raise their families and be housewives and not to pursue a career outside the home. Being a full-time mom can be a rewarding experience, but like all things in life, it can also have its pitfalls. Often, such women have difficulty asking for things for themselves.

If this describes you, it is probably due to the following two reasons. First, you were trained *not* to think of yourself; you were taught to take care of others first and your own needs last. The result is usually that you have little, if any, energy left over for yourself. Second, the members of your family see you in a certain way and don't want you to change. They may resist your growing from a person who always takes care of *them* to a person who also takes care of *herself*.

The kinds of self-awarenesses and strength-building I am talking about can be difficult to achieve by yourself, so you may well benefit from some help. Get together with friends and talk about these issues. Or consider joining a women's support group. Whatever you do, remember that you *do* deserve things for yourself and you *can* have them.

The situation for men is less clear-cut but just as difficult. Most men are not taught to be caregivers; instead, they are taught to be assertive or aggressive and to take what they want for themselves. But much of this is superficial. Most men also have a hard time standing up for themselves and believing that they have a right to get things for themselves—especially things like privacy and love.

The other troublesome personality trait I want to discuss is the desire to avoid arguments at all costs. Some parents will do almost anything to prevent a conflict or a fight between them and their children. But this is only part of the story, because in almost every case what these parents are really avoiding is any kind of *confrontation* with their children. Many people have difficulty seeing the differences between a conflict and a confrontation; to them the two situations look and feel the same. And since the two words are often mistakenly thought to be synonymous, a confrontation has very negative connotations. But to confront does not necessarily mean to conflict. To confront literally means to meet face to face, to oppose, or to set side by side for purposes of comparison. To conflict, on the other hand, means to fight or battle. While a confrontation can be merely a meeting, a conflict is always a disagreement. Applying these definitions to the subject at hand, we can state that confrontation is a part of every rule-making situation while conflict may or may not be.

Whenever you make a rule, you are meeting your children face to face and telling them what you want them to do. You are setting *your* idea of what they should do alongside *their* idea of what they should do. This is really what it means to confront. Since confrontation is a valid and integral part of the rule-making process, you cannot avoid it if you want to be successful.

Of course it's not always possible to avoid a certain amount of conflict during a confrontation. No matter how much love and respect you and your children have for each other, and no matter how good you are at making and carrying out rules, things will not always go smoothly. Some rules will be unpopular and may indeed lead to conflict. But conflict is *not* an inevitable outcome of the rule-making process.

Confronting others, your children or other adults, is unpleasant because it causes everyone involved to experience stress (although not as much stress as a serious argument or conflict). Sometimes the stress manifests itself physiologically—for example, in sweaty palms or a general feeling of nervousness. Sometimes its effects are more psychological, causing a feeling of being "on the spot" or of being challenged. And because confrontation is a challenging situation, it can also produce feelings of inadequacy.

While it is not possible to eliminate all stress from confrontations, it is possible to greatly minimize it. At any rate, it is better to have a confrontation and experience some stress than it is to avoid confrontation entirely. Parents who do avoid confrontation with their children usually end up in the one situation they fear the most— an open conflict or outright argument. And this in turn produces even more stress.

What can you do to make confrontations easier? First, it helps to *be aware* that whenever you make rules or carry them out you *are* engaged in a confrontation. The next step is to expect to hear a certain amount of grumbling from your children and refuse to take it personally.

When you make an unpopular rule and your children complain, they are doing what we *all* do or feel like doing when someone tells us that we have to do something we don't want to do or can't do something we want to do. This is natural and should *not* be perceived as an attack on you as a worthwhile person. On the other hand, this doesn't mean that you have to ignore your feelings. No one likes to hear complaints or be the recipient of dirty looks. It's okay to acknowledge that growls and glares are unpleasant; it's not necessary to take them to heart.

Second, it helps to remind yourself that you are the *adult* in the rule-making situation. As the adult, you have the *right* to make rules and see that they are carried out.

Some parents fall into the trap of believing that being the adult means being perfect, and that unless they can make perfect rules they have no right to make any at all. But this way of thinking can have disastrous results. As soon as you start doubting your own capabilities as a parent, you are apt to begin backing down at the first sign of disagreement from your children. Being the adult means doing the best you can. Sometimes you will be wrong, and almost certainly you will sometimes make rotten rules, but these things happen to the best of parents.

Let's look at what happened to one parent who had a severe block against getting involved in confrontations.

THE FEAR OF SAYING NO: A CASE STUDY

Peter entered the ministry in response to the turmoil and strife he had experienced as a child and a teenager. He hoped that the church would give him the peace and tranquility he had never known.

Peter's father was an alcoholic who regularly took his alcoholic rages out on his family. Whenever Peter thought about his early life, his memories were always of the yelling and shouting and hitting that went on in his home.

A few years after he was ordained, Peter was given his own church and settled down to the life of a small-town clergyman. He soon became very popular. His door was always open, and he always seemed to have time for his parishioners. In time, though, he became aware of a problem in his apparently happy life. Although he enjoyed helping others, it seemed to him that the members of his congregation sometimes took advantage of him. But he just couldn't bring himself to say no to anyone. Besides, it *was* his job to be there to help.

A couple of years later, Peter married a woman named Alicia. Although the two of them decided to wait awhile before having children, Peter secretly hoped that it would take a long time. He felt vaguely that he was not cut out to be a parent. He liked children, and he enjoyed joining some of the children's activities sponsored by the church, but he wasn't at all sure he wanted any of his own.

When Alicia announced that she was pregnant, Peter quieted his doubts. Maybe being a parent wouldn't be so bad after all, he thought. And he didn't want to do anything to spoil his wife's happiness. They had a son and, two years after that, another.

When he and Alicia talked about how they were going to raise their children, they decided that they would make as few rules as possible. In this way Peter hoped to provide the kind of loving atmosphere for *his* children that he himself had never had. Most important, he vowed to himself that there would never be any arguing or yelling in their house.

All went well until his oldest son Brian turned two years old and began to behave in very negative ways. Peter and Alicia met their son's negativeness with as much acceptance as they could. Peter reasoned that if they just let Brian be negative he would eventually "get it out of his system." So they did nothing to stop him and set virtually no rules to guide his behavior.

But Brian did not get his negative behavior out of his system. In fact, he got worse over the next several years until finally he refused to do *anything* his parents asked.

Peter tried to reason with his son, but Brian would have none of that. Finally both parents decided that some rules would have to be instituted. But at the first sign that his behavior was about to be restricted, Brian threw a tantrum and his parents backed off. Actually, Alicia was in favor of sticking with the rules a little longer, but Peter couldn't stand the thought of the yelling and the screaming that would inevitably follow.

Peter was unable to come up with an answer to the problem. And, to make matters worse, he was beginning to feel angry much of the time. Worse yet, he was *staying* angry. This frightened him very much. He had nightmares of physically hurting his son—and he began to wonder if he was really any different from his own father.

COMMENTS ON THE CASE STUDY

Peter had a serious problem with confrontations and conflicts. His own childhood had been so traumatic that as an adult he was desperate to avoid anything that even resembled a faceoff or an argument. He couldn't say no to his parishioners or to his own child because he feared what might happen.

So Peter became an overly permissive parent. Ironically, by his over-permissiveness he created the very situation he had tried so hard to avoid and was so afraid of—a family in which there was a great deal of anger.

Before Peter could learn to deal realistically with Brian's behavior, he had to learn to deal with his *own* feelings about anger. Perhaps because of his early experiences, he looked at the expression of *any* anger as an evil thing. Anger meant hitting and abusing; this was the pattern his father had established. Peter couldn't accept the fact that he might still be angry at his father, or that there might be times when it was okay for him to be angry at Brian or for Brian to be angry at him.

What does this mean for you as a parent? In order to work through a block of this kind, is it always necessary to go back to your childhood and dig up the conflicts and the memories? Probably not. Sometimes it's enough to realize that you have such a block and then take small steps toward changing your behavior.

But if this doesn't work for you, it may be necessary to go back into your past and do some uncovering. This can be very painful, so be sure to proceed slowly. Some professional counseling might be useful at this time.

****

Often when parents come in and talk to me about the problems they have getting their children to follow the rules, they'll say something like this: "Everything goes okay until my kids question the rules or argue with me. When this happens *I* start to argue, too, and then it's all over."

What's wrong with arguing with your children about the rules? It's really very simple: As soon as you get into an argument about a rule, you are signifying to your children that *the rule is still open for discussion.* You may not see it this way, but this is the way your children will see it. And because the rule is still open for discussion, your children won't really be sure what is expected of them. They will also hold out the hope, however slim, that they won't have to follow the rule at all. So as soon as you start arguing, you can be almost positive that your children will be happy to join in.

It is frustrating when your children don't follow the rules or abide by the limits you have set. It may even make you angry, especially if you have stated a particular rule more than once. It's okay to have these feelings and it's okay—even desirable—to communicate them. But you can do this without arguing. Let's look at some examples.

You have stated twice that it's time for bed, but your child has made no move to comply. You are beginning to feel frustrated and angry, so you say, "I am getting very frustrated that you are not following the rule about bedtime."

That's a genuine sharing of your feelings, but it's *not* the same as arguing. Incidentally, it's also valuable feedback for your child; sometimes all you need to do to get children to follow rules is to let them know that you are angry or frustrated.

Compare the above response with this one: "Look, I've told you three times that it's time for bed. You know how cranky you are in the morning if you don't get enough sleep. What would happen if I let you stay up late every night?"

Now *this* is arguing. Instead of expressing your frustration in a straightforward way, you are inviting your child to take

part in a fruitless discussion about an impossible situation—
staying up late every night.

Arguing isn't much fun, nor is it very productive, but
it generally isn't a problem unless it becomes chronic—that
is, unless it happens most of the time. We all have days
when, for whatever reason, we have a very low tolerance
for being disagreed with. If you find yourself having a day
like this, you may also find yourself arguing about rules
more than you usually do. Just don't let it happen too
frequently!

Perhaps you only argue about one rule and the rest go
smoothly. The problem here may be that you have made a
rule you are not comfortable with and this is leading to
arguments. Or perhaps you are trying to enforce a rule
about a behavior or activity that is best left unstructured.
An occasional isolated incident of this type is not a cause
for undue concern.

If you *do* find yourself arguing frequently, you probably
need to redirect your energy away from arguing and back
into yourself to find out what is going on there. Take time
to get in touch with your own feelings and the reasons
behind them. And you may discover that often when you
argue about rules, you are really trying to *convince* or
persuade your children that what you are doing is right. You
want them on your side. You want them to agree with you.

The key, then, is to examine that part of you that *feels
it necessary* to persuade or convince rather than to hold
firm. Listen to yourself when you argue. What emotional
quality does your voice have? Do you sound scared?
Unsure? Are you pleading, hoping your kids will take
mercy on you? Do you sound angry or harsh? If so, might
this be a cover-up for some other feeling? Are you sounding
angry when you are really feeling scared?

Once you have identified your emotional state, it is
easier to discover the specific attitude that is causing you to
try to persuade or convince your children rather than to be
firm with them. One attitude I have often noticed in my

work with parents is this: The parents try to get things—friendship, respect, love, etc.—from their children because they feel they cannot get these things from other adults. Frequently, these parents feel lonely and isolated except for their children. Given this need to have their children on their side, these parents will be careful not to do anything to alienate them. They will not make unpopular rules or, if they do, they won't carry them out. Indeed, they will have difficulty being firm about *anything* in their lives.

Of course, this description is rather extreme; every parent acts like this *to a certain extent*, but few do so all the time. It's only when it happens constantly that you need to be concerned. It's natural for parents to want their children to like them; it becomes a problem only if you become *dependent* on your children for most of the affection in your life and cannot tolerate the thought that they may not like you.

Another topic that always comes up during any discussion of rules is that of discipline. This is an area in which many parents feel confused or at a loss. You may be surprised to learn that most dictionary definitions of the word discipline have nothing to do with punishment. Most deal with the issues of training or control, including self-control. In my dictionary, punishment is listed only in the last definition, where discipline is defined as treatment that corrects *or* punishes.

I believe that children need to be disciplined when they break a rule or fail to observe a limit. But discipline should *not* be used to hurt children or to assert the parents' strength. Instead, it should have this as its goal: making sure that the children follow the rule the next time.

Assuming that your family's rules are reasonable and have been properly set up, your children should understand that something unpleasant will happen if they don't follow them. The question is, what unpleasant consequence will you choose? Disapproval? Physical punishment? Loss of privileges?

In most cases, the only consequence needed is your verbal disapproval. In my experience, this works 60 to 70 percent of the time. When you tell your children that you are frustrated or angry when they aren't following the rules, your disapproval becomes a form of discipline—often the only form that's needed.

Perhaps you think that your kids don't really care whether you approve of their behavior or not, so showing your disapproval won't have much effect. But most of the time your kids *do* care. As a general rule, children want their parents' approval very much, and parental *disapproval* can be terribly upsetting to them.

Two factors make it difficult for parents to see the usefulness of this approach. First, children often do not show that they care about parental approval, even though they really do. This is especially true of older children and adolescents—it's just not "cool" to let on that they care one way or another what Mom or Dad thinks of them. Second, many parents make the mistake of being in too much of a hurry when using this approach.

Let's look at some examples illustrating this situation. You find your five-year-old giving a tea party with your best china. He knows that there is a rule prohibiting this. You begin by saying, "Mark, I want you to stop playing with those dishes." Mark makes no response. So you continue by saying, "Mark, I do not want you to play with those dishes. You have dishes of your own to play with." Mark still makes no response. Finally you say, "I don't like what you are doing and I'm getting angry." Then you wait to see what happens. After a few seconds Mark gives you a worried look and puts the dishes down. You have gotten him to do what you want without too much conflict. Notice too that you have given him an *alternative* to playing with your best china—a very effective tactic.

Now consider this series of responses to the same

situation.

You say, "Mark, I want you to stop playing with those dishes." Mark makes no response. So, with your voice rising, you say, "Mark, I mean it when I say that I don't want you to play with those dishes. I don't like what you are doing at all. It's making me angry and if you don't stop *right now* I'm going to spank you!" Mark hurriedly puts the dishes down.

You have gotten him to do what you want, all right, but how? You haven't given him enough time to react to the statement of your disapproval, and you have added the threat of a spanking.

Disapproval will work only if you give your child enough time and space to decide what he or she wants to do about it. An effective technique is to *stop* with the statement of your disapproval and don't add *anything*. Be patient. Count to five or even ten. It's also important to pay attention to your body language; even though you don't say anything, your body may be stiff and tense, and your child may interpret this to mean that you are about to take some action rather than waiting for him or her to make a decision.

What are the consequences of threatening a spanking? First, if your child decides to obey you, you won't know whether it was because of your disapproval or the threat of more violent discipline. Second, you are digging a hole for yourself, because if your child doesn't obey, you will probably feel committed to following through on your threat to spank him or her.

It takes patience to discipline with disapproval. If you are not a patient person, if you **want** things to happen right away, you may have some special difficulties here. But you *can* do it. It's primarily a matter of self-control. Counting really helps. Say the numbers to yourself in your head, or take a few deep breaths. However you do it, the goal is for you to put some psychological and even some physical distance between you and your child.

This technique will work in most instances. But what if it doesn't? In general, I am against the use of physical punishment such as spanking and ear-tweaking. It's not necessary, and it's humiliating to your child. And since most parents use physical punishment when they are angry or frustrated, they are teaching their children that it's okay to hit or hurt someone when *they* are angry or frustrated. Another reason not to use physical punishment is that it only works because—and as long as—you are the bigger and stronger one. Even though it *seems* to work when children are young (because they fear you), it will usually *not* work when they reach adolescence. At that point, you will be in big trouble—I guarantee it.

If you have to use some form of discipline other than your disapproval, make it something that involves the least possible amount of coercion. Remember that your goal is to correct mistakes, not to bully. For example:

Your children are not following the dinnertime rules. You repeat them several times and let your children know that you are getting frustrated, but you get no response. So you say, "Since you can't behave at the dinner table, you'll have to eat by yourselves in the kitchen tonight." Then you pick up their dishes, guide them into the kitchen, and go back to finishing your own dinner.

It's also important, especially for young children, to make discipline as immediate as possible. In the above example, it would be a *mistake* to say, "If you don't follow the dinnertime rules, you won't be able to eat with us tomorrow night." This is too far in the future to have much meaning for children.

Discipline should not only be immediate, it should also have some logical connection to the situation at hand. For example, it makes sense to remove a misbehaving child from the dinner table because that's where the problem is taking place. It would be much less effective to say, "If you can't behave at the table, I won't read you a bedtime story."

In this case the connection between the misconduct and the discipline would be far less clear.

To discipline in this manner takes time—time to state the rules, and time to communicate your own feelings. But there are instances when more rapid action is necessary. If your children are about to hurt one another or themselves or you, you may not have time for words. In these cases I believe it's best to use firm but gentle restraint.

I remember an incident that occurred during the first session I had with one five-year-old girl. We were about to start play therapy, and I had just finished stating the rules, one of which was that I did not want her to do anything that would injure me. Almost immediately she took a can of open paint and, with a mischievous grin, held it over my head. I had two choices: I could state the rule again, or I could take the paint can away from her. I chose to take the paint can!

What often happens when parents try to become more effective at rule-making is that they learn the techniques, gain some self-awareness, and then get into a situation where nothing seems to work. This is very discouraging, but it's also normal, and it will probably happen more times than you care to think about. It's hard to break old patterns and learn new ones.

Give yourself time. Celebrate your small advances. And, most important, give yourself credit for trying new things even if they don't pay off right away.

In the beginning, it might be a good idea to put your energy into a single rule or limit rather than trying to change them all. You might even pick a rule that is already working fairly well and make it better. In this way you can learn what it feels like to be successful, and your success will give you the strength to persist, even during very difficult times.

IV. DEALING WITH FAMILY CHANGES

Every family undergoes changes. Basically, there are three kinds. First are the changes that occur every day as part of the daily family routine. These are the *transition times*. A transition time is any instance in which one activity is stopped and another begun. Mealtimes, bedtimes, getting up in the morning, and going to school or work are all times when children and adults must make the transition from one activity to another.

Second are the *age-related changes* that every child goes through. These include advancing from one grade to another, graduating from elementary school to junior high, and going through the physical and emotional changes that come with adolescence. (See Chapter Ten, Coping with Adolesence.)

The third kind of change is not built into the family structure, although almost every family goes through one or two changes of this type. I call these *episodic changes* and they include such incidents as moving from one locality to another, times when adults change jobs, and alterations in the composition of the family due to divorce or remarriage.

Changes can be very difficult for children, as well as adults, to deal with. When we go through a change we move from a *known* place—whether psychological or physical or both—to a relatively *unknown* one, and the unknown can be frightening. Whenever we move into unfamiliar territory, we aren't sure what to expect and we aren't sure whether we will be able to control and order and make sense out of our new experiences.

The negative aspects of change can be lessened by careful *preparation*. A metaphor I like to use is that of constructing a bridge between the familiar and the unfamiliar. It's very important to prepare *yourself* as well as your children for expected changes, since your family is a system in which something that is felt by one person is bound to be felt by all.

Let's illustrate this with an example of how one family dealt with an episodic change.

BACK TO WORK: A CASE STUDY

Anne's life was a comfortable one. Her husband David had a good job in the aerospace industry and he brought home enough money that Anne did not have to work outside the home.

They had two children, Shawna, four, and Tony, five. Although both children were old enough for preschool, their parents decided not to enroll them. The time for school would come soon enough. Besides, Anne liked having her children home with her.

Then David lost his job. He was eventually rehired, but only on a half-time basis. This placed a heavy drain on the family savings, and in a few months it was obvious to Anne that she would have to find a job.

David and Anne were intelligent parents, and they realized that Anne's return to work would have a profound impact on their children. In particular, Tony and Shawna might have some problems adjusting to Anne's not being there during the day and to being left with a sitter. The parents spent many hours talking about how they would deal with this.

Anne also talked about her own feelings. She felt sad and a little frightened at the thought of leaving her children with a sitter for so much of the day. David shared her concern, so together, Anne and David discussed ways to prepare for the change in their lives.

A few weeks before she was to begin work, Anne started leaving the children with sitters for increasingly longer periods of time. She also explained to them that there would come a time when she would be gone most of the day.

As the experiment proceeded, the children developed some concerns and fears. Anne and David took the time to listen carefully to them. On the day Anne began her job, the children said goodbye without any fuss.

COMMENTS ON THE CASE STUDY

The approach Anne and David took to their change was a very constructive one. By leaving the children with a sitter for increasingly longer periods of time, they were in effect *rehearsing* for the real thing. This approach allowed the children to get used to the idea gradually. In addition, the talking Anne and David did between themselves about what impact the change might have on their children and about their own feelings as parents—was also a kind of rehearsal. They not only prepared their children, but they prepared themselves, too. And when the big day arrived, everyone was ready.

****

It isn't always possible to prepare for a change in such a thorough way. It isn't always possible to set up a real situation and have the leisure to experiment with it. For certain kinds of changes, this approach might not be at all practical or possible. But the same results can be achieved by using another method: the role play.

Role playing is a useful and effective way to prepare yourself and your children for most episodic changes. It is also useful in approaching some age-related changes, especially those involving school.

A role play is a make-believe situation in which each person involved plays a certain role or part. It is much like a real play. The difference is that role playing is done for specific reasons; namely, to help the players experience certain feelings and attitudes which they will need in order to act the part in real life.

If you have ever scheduled a job interview, you may have used role playing to get ready for it. You may have talked in front of a mirror, rehearsing what you were going to say. Or you may have asked another person to play the part of your prospective employer while you played yourself. And you may have even switched roles. By doing these things you became aware of the feelings you were likely to have in the real interview, especially those feelings that could work against you. After exploring these feelings, you were better able to do something to correct them. Perhaps in the role play you could spot times when you got nervous and practice those parts until you worked out your nervousness.

Role playing helps us prepare for change because it is a low-risk way of experiencing the newness that change brings. Since it's only make-believe, faltering or stumbling isn't as frightening or as damaging to our egos as it is in real life. We can laugh and joke about our mistakes and, in this way, relieve some of the anxiety change often brings.

Children adapt very readily to role plays, probably because they naturally use this technique as a way to experiment with new situations and roles. Preschoolers who "play school" are using role playing to prepare for their new roles as students.

How do you role play a change situation? How do you set it up? Let's use the situation from the preceding case study to illustrate some answers.

Step One: Anne and David explain to Shawna and
             Tony that Mommy is going back to work in
             two weeks. They tell them that she will be
             gone from 8:00 in the morning until 5:00 in
             the afternoon and that while she is away a
             babysitter will take care of them. Afterward
             the children voice some questions and fears,

and Anne and David acknowledge them and talk about them.

Step Two: Anne and David set the stage for the role play by saying, "Now we're going to play a game. We're going to pretend that it's 7:30 in the morning and Mommy is going to work. We've just finished eating breakfast, and the babysitter is about to knock on the door."

Step Three: The family goes through the role play, with David playing the part of the babysitter.

Step Four: Everyone talks about what it felt like to go through the experience.

It's important that you get something for *yourself* when you role play, by the way. It shouldn't just be something you do for your children.

Rehearsing and role playing are both good techniques to use when preparing your family for an episodic change. But what can you do to make transition times easier? These changes, during which one activity is stopped and another started, occur every day in every family. And they can be very troublesome.

Many parents complain that no matter what they do, they cannot get their kids ready for school in the morning. Or they cannot get them to quiet down at night in time to go to sleep. The same kinds of complaints are heard about other transition times. Why are these so difficult, and what can you do about them?

To begin with, it helps to step back and take a wider view of the situation. We all, children *and* adults, must deal with transitions in our daily lives and, although it may seem that only children have problems with transitions, this is not the case. Adults have problems, too, but the adult problems are not as obvious because adults have ways of coping with transitions that aren't available to children.

Some adults use drugs. The cup of coffee and the cigarette in the morning, the drink before dinner, and the sleeping pill at night are all ways to ease through transitions. Luckily, children don't usually have these options! In a more positive and constructive vein, adults generally learn to be self-regulating. As an adult you get yourself up in the morning and get ready for work because no one else will do it for you. Closer inspection shows that this kind of self-regulation is seldom a matter of free choice but rather a result of social pressure or fear. Even when you don't want to get up and go to work, you do it anyway because you are supposed to and you may be fired if you don't.

Children have not learned this kind of self-regulation, however. Unlike adults, they do not feel the need to respond to social pressure. Although children tend to be creatures of habit, they do *not* tend to be creatures of schedule, and I believe that they genuinely have trouble understanding why adults are so insistent on always doing certain things at certain times. Children resist being scheduled, and this makes transition times difficult for them.

Coping successfully with transition times is a learning process for children and parents alike. There are three things you can do to make your job easier: getting *yourself* ready to help your children through transition times; realizing that transition times are difficult for children and that you can expect to have some problems; and learning how to cue your children that *they* need to get ready for a particular transition. Let's talk about the third tactic first.

Although transition times are not as momentous as episodic changes, they have one important similarity: they both benefit from preparation. One way to prepare your children for transition times is to *cue* them. I'll give an example of what I mean by this.

It's almost dinnertime and your kids are busy playing. You want to give them some kind of notice that a change in the schedule is coming soon, so you say,

"You have five more minutes to play, and then it will be time for dinner." This cue helps your children to prepare for the transition. (With very young children you might want to use a shorter time interval—say two or three minutes instead of five.)

No matter how much time you give your children to prepare for a transition, it is important that this be *free time*. When you use a cue, you are telling your children that they can do what they want for a certain amount of time and then they must stop. If you say something like, "Dinner in five minutes, go and wash up," you will be defeating the purpose of the cue because the fact that they must wash means that the five-minute interval is not really theirs to do with as they please.

Getting yourself ready—the first tactic I mentioned earlier—is also important because helping your children through a transition time creates a transition time for you, too. You must stop whatever you are doing—cooking, resting, etc.—and begin a different task; namely, getting your children to make a transition. So cue *yourself* that you will be making the change by giving yourself a couple of minutes to get ready. If one or two minutes isn't long enough, take more time. Sometimes no matter how much time you take you won't be ready to make the shift; if this happens, try to switch with your partner and have him or her get the kids ready.

Finally, you should expect that you are probably going to have *some* problems effecting transitions. No matter how well you have cued yourself and your children, they are likely to resist making the transition. You will be more successful if you can develop a tolerance for a certain amount of grumbling and complaining. It's especially important not to take this personally.

If you're going to have problems, they will probably arise during the first couple of minutes after a new activity is begun. Children often need time to adjust to a new activity, and they're seldom very quiet while they're doing it! Oftentimes you can deal with this fussing and squirming with a gentle reminder of what is expected. But if things look as if they are going to get out of hand, it's important that you deal with the situation immediately.

If gentle reminders do not work, some kind of discipline is necessary. Remember, a firm, clear message of your disapproval will work in most cases. If not, make the discipline as logical and as immediate as possible.

V. HANDLING FAMILY CONFLICTS

Every family has *some* conflicts, since what pleases one family member may not please another. Younger family members may not like certain rules and will argue about them. They aren't the only ones, of course. Husbands and wives will argue about money, about how to raise the kids, and about how they should relate to each other. Arguments can arise over almost any issue.

Although every family experiences conflicts, each deals with them in different ways. Some families are open about conflicts; they argue or fight or in some other way make their disagreements known to one another. Other families are not as open and keep their differences to themselves. They may even act as if there is a rule which forbids them from airing complaints. And often there *is* such a rule, although it is never openly acknowledged.

In general, families who do not bring their conflicts out in the open have farther to go before they can resolve their differences. When people aren't willing to talk or argue, there is no starting place for the resolution process. This is only a generalization, of course; families who fight openly may get no farther than families who don't. Sometimes open fighting is a way to *avoid* dealing with differences and resolving them.

What I am saying here is that every family—including yours—experiences some conflict. But how much is normal?

I feel that a certain amount of conflict is healthy. Conflict can be one way of expressing individuality, of saying what *you* want, of finding out who *you* are. Conflict is also a signal that family members' needs aren't being met, and it can point the way to unresolved or hidden issues, indicating areas in which work needs to be done.

But not *all* conflict is healthy. Although there is no

hard and fast principle one can use to measure this, a good rule of thumb is that conflict is destructive when it becomes chronic and goes on and on without ever being resolved.

Let's look at what one family did to resolve a conflict that was becoming chronic.

THE "PERFECT MARRIAGE": A CASE STUDY

When Ed and Susan got married, they believed that their marriage would last forever. They seemed to share the same dreams. They didn't talk much about their dreams—only enough to convince themselves that there really were no serious differences in the way they saw things or in the things they wanted.

Their three children were very close in age. Jason was eight years old, Sherri was seven, and Terri was five. The family had everything going for it...or at least it seemed that way on the outside.

But Ed and Susan were growing further and further apart from each other. At first the problem didn't seem serious, but it gradually escalated to the point where each felt as if the other was a stranger. They avoided talking about it because they felt that talking about it would make it more real, and they were both afraid of what was happening.

And they were both angry, although they had no one to be angry at. Secretly they felt disappointed, as if life were somehow cheating them out of a promise. Things progressed to a point where they rarely spoke to each other at all. It seemed like too much of an effort.

Then Terri started wetting her bed at night. Susan was confused, because none of her children had ever been bed-wetters. She took her daughter to a doctor, but he could find nothing physically wrong.

Sherri and Jason also started having problems. They were cranky and uncooperative most of the time, and they fought and complained about almost everything.

Ed suggested that it was time to start being stricter with the children. Susan agreed, although she privately doubted that it was the right thing to do. Both parents began spanking the children, something they had never done in the past.

Then Susan began losing her temper several times a day with her children, often over trivial things. She found herself spanking them harder than she really meant to. She felt scared and guilty.

Finally she made arrangements to see a counselor and convinced Ed to accompany her. The counselor suggested that they acknowledge the fact that they had problems in their marriage. She also suggested that they level with their children about this.

Ed and Susan took the counselor's advice. They began to talk about the difficulties they were experiencing. They even fought once in a while. And they talked with their children. They shared at least some of what was going on between them.

Almost immediately, the children's behavior changed. Terri stopped wetting the bed, and Sherri and Jason stopped being uncooperative and cranky.

COMMENTS ON THE CASE STUDY

This case shows clearly how families work as systems and how disturbances in one part of the family will eventually affect everyone. In this particular case, the conflict between the parents spread to the children, affecting them *and* the parent-child relationships.

The relationship between marriage partners sets the tone for the life of the family, and in general, if parents leave differences unresolved at the beginning of their marriage, they will usually show up later and will almost certainly affect any children they have. This is not the same as saying that the parents are at fault; only that they have some work to do.

The source of the conflict in Ed and Susan's family was probably the unspoken expectations and assumptions the two of them had of each other and of their marriage. They each expected that certain things would happen and that the other person would want the same things. When this did not go according to plan, both Ed and Susan experienced a sense of separateness which eventually resulted in conflict. Expectations and assumptions that are not talked about are like time bombs—they may go off at any moment with disastrous results.

Before they started seeing the counselor, Ed and Susan followed an unspoken rule that they were not to fight about their disagreements. Since they themselves were trying to keep such a tight lid on their differences, it might seem surprising that their children's behavior was affected. But children always know when their parents are experiencing stresses and strains. They may not know what the issues are, and they may be too young to understand the issues even if they are explained, but they *know* when things aren't right. And, in the absence of any specific information, children will draw their *own* conclusions. Often they will believe that the conflict is worse than it really is, or that one or both parents is about to leave, or that *they* are to blame for their parents' problems. The result is usually increased anxiety or fear and maladaptive behavior. Maladaptive behavior—temper tantrums, rule-breaking, etc.—is sometimes the only way for children to deal with anxiety they are experiencing.

Children can usually tolerate parental conflict *as long as they know what is going on.* As soon as Ed and Susan began to be more open with their children about their problems, the children's maladaptive behavior stopped. If there is a lesson to be learned from this case, it is this: It's almost *always* best for parents to acknowledge the differences between themselves and share some of this with their children.

If your family is experiencing conflict, it helps if you

can identify the real issues involved. This is not as easy as it sounds, however. Often what *seems* to be a real issue isn't, or it may be only part of a real issue.

Whenever you peel one layer off of an onion, you're almost sure to find another underneath. It's the same with family conflicts, especially those that have been going on for a long time. You don't have to remove *all* the layers, but the more you take off the better your chances are for a genuine resolution.

Unfortunately, family conflicts are often very complicated, and to uncover the real source of a problem can be time-consuming. It's too easy to go off in wrong directions. This can be frustrating, and it sometimes helps to get an outsider's point of view, perhaps that of a friend or a counselor.

In the case of Ed and Susan's family, there were actually *two* situations causing conflict at the same time: the parents' inability to communicate, and the children's maladaptive behavior. But the *real* issue was between the parents. If they had continued to concentrate their efforts on trying to settle the conflict between themselves and their children, they would have had little success because that situation was only a byproduct of the one that existed between the two of them. Where they needed to begin, and where they in fact did begin, was with the issues that were separating them as a couple.

Once you have decided where to begin approaching a conflict, the single factor that will do the most to determine whether it is resolved is *the point of view of those involved in the conflict.* Your point of view—your attitude—is crucial, because it will determine what you and other family members are willing to do about a conflict.

The most productive point of view for family members to take is for each person to see himself or herself as part of the process, part of the problem, and part of the solution; in other words, to see the conflict as "our" problem rather than "their" problem or "his" problem or "her" problem.

When family members see a conflict as "our" problem, there is less need to place blame or to try to figure out who is "right" and who is "wrong." Placing blame or being preoccupied with right and wrong will hinder any meaningful solution. Blaming others is a way of putting oneself *outside* the system. It builds walls, and walls prevent real dialogue.

When family members see a conflict as "our" problem, they are much more willing to disclose important information about themselves. This is crucial because conflicts cannot be resolved unless those involved are willing to share their feelings, fears, expectations, and assumptions. Resolving conflicts takes trust. People will *not* trust one another if they feel that they are being examined to determine their guilt. Nor will they trust one another if they feel that other family members are unwilling to share themselves.

I'm going to give some examples of what I mean by this, but first I would like you to do a brief exercise that will help to make the examples more useful to you. Find a piece of paper and a pencil, settle into a quiet corner (unless, of course, there *are* no quiet corners in your home—which is a problem you should be dealing with!), and write down *your* view of the conflicts that are taking place in your family right now. You don't have to do anything with them, although it might be useful to compare your views with the examples below. (Don't read these until *after* you finish doing the exercise.)

The following statements illustrate how some "typical" family members might view conflict situations:

Man: "When I come home at night, my kids are always after me to do things. I wish they would stop. Can't they see how tired I am?"

Woman: "My children are all grown, and I'd like to go back to work. But my family is not giving me the support I need, and I resent that."

Both   "Our children aren't doing well in school. They
Parents: don't listen when we tell them how important
           school is to their future."

Teenage   "I try to get my homework done every day when
Child: I get home from school, but Mom and Dad are
           always asking me to do something around the
           house. They say I can get everything done, but I
           don't see how."

In each of these examples, conflict is always somebody
else's fault. The speakers seem to feel as if they have no
part in the conflict except as victims. And the only *feelings*
they are sharing are frustration and anger over what *others*
are doing *to* them.

With a better understanding of the attitudes they need
in order to resolve their conflicts, these people might sound
like this:

Man: "I don't particularly like my job; it's a dead end.
           When I come home I carry some of this
           frustration with me and I guess sometimes I resent
           having my family put demands on me."

Woman: "I'd like to go back to work, but I'm not really
           sure. What if I can't make it in today's job
           market? I feel pretty insecure about the whole
           thing, and I guess sometimes I'd like my family to
           say that everything would be okay and that I'd be
           great. I know that wouldn't be the answer, but I'd
           still like them to say it, and I'm disappointed
           when they don't."

Both   "Neither one of us did very well in school, and
Parents: maybe that's why we don't have the kind of life
           we'd like to have. We'd like our kids to do better
           than we did, to have some of the things we don't

have. I guess that's one of the reasons we push
them."

Teenage   "I hate doing stuff around the house. It really puts
Child: me in a bad mood. And maybe that's why I can't
           listen to Mom and Dad when they try to show
           me how I can do my homework and my chores."

This is a very different set of examples from the first
one. Gone is the accusatory tone; these people are *not*
standing outside the system and pointing the finger of
blame at someone else. Rather, they are acknowledging that
they are part of their conflict. By getting in touch with some
of their deeper feelings and including themselves in the
process, they are opening the door for others to respond in
a similar manner. Notice, too, that the people in the second
set of examples avoid the equally disastrous mistake of
blaming themselves, which can be just as unproductive as
blaming others.

In order to work through conflicts, you sometimes
need to develop an awareness of certain things about
yourself. But it's equally important to realize that a conflict
is everyone's concern.

There are times, of course, when family conflicts
cannot be resolved by making changes within the family.
After all, families are not self-contained units. They're part
of a larger society and are affected by what goes on in it. In
certain kinds of conflicts, it is important to take this into
account. For instance, a family in which one of the adults
is out of work may experience conflict because unemployed
adults often have lower limits for tolerating stress. It may be
unrealistic to approach a conflict of this sort as if the
answer can be found within the family itself. While it may
be useful to work on such conflicts within the family
system, it is also wise to recognize that at least part of the
answer may lie *outside* the system. In this example, a *real*
resolution may not occur until the parent finds another
job.

When I first began my work in family therapy, I believed that all family problems could be solved if the family members had the desire to work them out and if they had the necessary skills or were willing to learn them. Certainly this is true in many cases, and hopefully families in trouble will continue to try to work out their problems. However, I have also come to believe that some people should simply not be married to each other, or perhaps to anyone. And I feel that some couples should not have children. But what happens if two incompatible people get married or have children when this isn't right for them?

The only answer may be to admit, without blaming anyone, that the present arrangement is not working and that the best thing to do is for the family to break apart. This can be a wrenching experience, but it is almost always preferable to staying together in an atmosphere of chronic conflict and mutually destructive relationships.

Parents who contemplate such moves frequently feel tremendous guilt. They are sure that they have "failed" in some way. This is especially true when parents are thinking of giving up their children. This kind of guilt is often reinforced by social norms, for society can be a harsh critic.

To my mind, though, this is backwards thinking. To me, the ability to let go of a damaging relationship is a sign of great strength and courage. It is also a way to demonstrate *real* love and *real* concern.

VI. THE "PROBLEM CHILD"

If you have a "problem child," you may already have made the rounds—to doctors, psychologists, and school officials—in an attempt to find out *why* your child is having difficulties. This can be time-consuming, costly, and frustrating, for often the end result is that you have no clearer idea of what is wrong or what to do than when you began.

I have no easy answers to give you. I wish I did, because I have treated many families who have "problem children," and I know the turmoil and pain this often entails.

A "problem child" is a child or an adolescent who is experiencing severe emotional and/or behavioral difficulties. Sometimes these difficulties seem to be confined to only one or two areas of the child's life; for instance, a child may have problems at school but none at home. Usually, though, all areas of the child's life are adversely affected.

A "problem child" or adolescent often holds a unique place in the family in the sense that he or she stands out as being the one with the *most* problems. Sometimes he or she may seem to be the *only* family member with problems, and the parents and others in the family will describe him or her in this way.

The parents of such a child are often mystified as to *why* one of their children should be so troubled. They say something like, "I just can't understand it; I've done everything I can and nothing works; I'm at the end of my rope." Whenever I hear a parent say this I sigh inwardly, because I know that if I work with that family for any length of time I will almost certainly have to tell them some things they do not want to hear.

Specifically, the "problem child" is a product of a

family that is *itself* having problems. He or she becomes the focus for the difficulties the family as a whole is having and the vehicle through which these difficulties and conflicts are expressed.

If you own a pressure cooker, you know that there is a safety mechanism that allows the steam to escape before dangerous amounts of pressure can build up. Families can be like pressure cookers; the pressures build up inside and threaten to blow the family apart. The "problem child" acts as a kind of safety valve for the family. Family members let off steam through him or her. But this is hardly an efficient or healthy way for families to deal with conflict.

There are a few exceptions to what I have been saying. Sometimes children have physical problems that result in behavioral disorders. A thorough physical is therefore a wise place to start if your child is having emotional or behavioral difficulties. In general, however, I believe that the "problem child" is made, not born. Let's examine this idea more closely by looking at another case study.

THE THREATENING MOVE: A CASE STUDY

Nothing had been normal around the Noble house for the past several weeks—ever since the day John Noble announced that he had been offered a promotion at almost double his current salary.

At first his news was met with glee by his wife Andrea and his two children. Then he had added that the new job was in a city 300 miles away, and *this* piece of news was not well received. Nobody liked the thought of moving, and the whole family had been arguing for weeks about what they were going to do.

John saw the new job as a great opportunity. It meant that his family could have some of the things that it had been impossible for him to provide in the past. And for him personally it meant an opportunity to advance in his field. He'd been waiting for a break like this for five years, and he was excited. He was also hurt that no one else seemed to share his excitement; after all, he was doing it for *them*, too. Sure, the move would mean some disruption for the family, but for John the positive aspects outweighed the negative ones.

Not for Andrea. She was numbed by the news. Of course she could see the obvious economic advantages, but that was the *only* good she could see in such a move.

The family had lived in the same house for seven years. This was their *home*. And what about Andrea's career? She was a research assistant in the psychology department of the local university, and in another year she would be in the doctoral program. She could go to school somewhere else, of course, but she had connections here, and moving would set her plans back several years.

She knew that John was excited, and a part of her was excited for him. Three or four years ago, she would have moved without much hesitation. But not now. Things were different now. It just wasn't right that he should ask everyone to move!

If Andrea was numb, twelve-year-old Christie was paralyzed. She couldn't believe that they were going to just pack up and move! And to that horrible city! She'd heard bad things about the schools there. She shuddered when she thought of going to a school where they had to have policemen patrolling the halls.

She wasn't going! She wasn't going to leave all her friends. She'd run away first—and she'd take her brother Timmy with her!

Timmy was seven years old. *He* didn't want to move either, although he didn't see what he could do about it. But what bothered him more than the thought of moving was that everyone was so angry all the time. He wanted them to stop yelling at each other. But he didn't see what he could do about that either, so he just kept quiet.

About a week after his father made the

announcement, Timmy started having bad dreams. He
didn't tell his parents about them, though; he didn't even
tell Christie. *

At the end of two weeks, tempers were short.
Although no one talked about it, they were all feeling the
same things. They were angry and confused. And each of
them felt that no one else was seeing *his* or *her* side of the
situation.

Over the next two weeks John and Andrea tried to
resolve their differences, but they never had any real
success. If anything, they came away from each encounter
even more confused and frustrated than they had been
before.

Another week passed. Then one Friday Andrea
received a call from the attendance secretary at Christie's
school. Christie hadn't been in class for the past week.
Andrea had trouble believing what she was hearing. She
thought that it must be some kind of joke—but it wasn't.

When her parents questioned her that night, Christie
freely admitted cutting classes, although she refused to say
where she had gone or why she had been skipping school.
She seemed proud of herself. Further questioning proved
useless.

Christie's behavior mystified her parents. It was so
unlike her; she had always enjoyed school, and she was one
of the top students. John and Andrea decided not to do
anything right away. They hoped that whatever was
bothering their daughter would simply "blow over."

But it didn't. Christie continued to cut classes, and the
school kept pressing John and Andrea to come up with
some answers.

The next few weeks saw a rather peculiar turn of
events. Andrea and John stopped fighting about whether or
not they were going to move. They seemed to forget all
about this conflict. Instead, they drew together and
concentrated their time and energy on helping Christie.

The two of them tried everything they could think of.

Andrea took time off from her university studies and had numerous talks with Christie's teachers and with other school personnel. She had long talks with Christie, too, although these were mostly monologues, since Christie contributed nothing to them. But none of this had much effect.

More out of frustration than anything else, John and Andrea decided to be stricter with Christie. Little by little, they took all of her privileges away. Andrea even began driving her to school in the morning and picking her up in the afternoon. Christie responded to this pressure by attending a few of her classes. As her teachers reported, though, she didn't do any work even when she was in class.

The subject of the move came up only once during this period. John said that his company had given him a deadline; he had several months to decide whether he would take the transfer and promotion. Except for that piece of news, the subject was not discussed.

Andrea had her own decisions to make. In order to have more time to help Christie, she had taken a temporary leave of absence from the university. But now her time was up and the professor she worked for was eager to have her back. This was a tribute to the skill with which she did her job, and at another time it would have pleased her to be needed so much, but now it didn't seem all that important. What *was* important was that she do everything she could to get Christie back on the right track. So she stalled the professor and hoped that he wouldn't give her job to someone else.

COMMENTS ON THE CASE STUDY

Imagine that you heard about this family at the point in time at which this case study ends—that is, when Christie is failing in school. You know *nothing* else about what is going on with them. What would you think?

You might be confused, because everyone in this family seems to be functioning reasonably well—*except for Christie*. From what you know, she is the *only* one who seems to be having problems. And Christie's parents are obviously concerned about her, which makes this situation even more confusing. It might be easier to understand Christie's behavior if her parents didn't care about her, but they *do* care, and they are exerting a great deal of energy in an attempt to help her. Christie's mother is even interrupting her own career in order to have more time for her daughter. It just seems like one of those things; sometimes even the best of families has a child who "goes wrong."

But if you were trained in family therapy, or if you had gone through something like this in your own family, you might be a little skeptical of the conclusion that Christie's behavior is "just one of those things." You might guess that there is something *else* going on in this family, some tension or conflict connected to Christie's school behavior. In order to discover what that tension or conflict is, though, you would need more information.

You might begin by working backwards in time until you came to the job offer and the commotion this caused in the family. Although the connection between *that* conflict and Christie's present behavior still might not be clear, this is nevertheless a good place to start.

When John first announced his news to the family, *everyone* was involved in the conflict caused by the impending move and the whole house was in an uproar. But then, little by little, the original conflict seemed to get pushed into the background as John and Andrea begin to deal with Christie's maladaptive behavior. The move to another city was apparently forgotten in light of the fact that Christie was on her way to becoming a "problem child." But what really happened here—and why?

Christie doesn't want to move to another city; she is angry and scared. Her negative behavior in school is her

way of expressing her anger and her fear. Certainly her
behavior is not really appropriate, and she might have
chosen a more direct way to reveal her feelings, but
children and adolescents often use acting-out behavior to
express their conflicts.

The real key to understanding this case lies in the fact
that the parents chose to deal with Christie's behavior,
which is a *symptom* of the original conflict, rather than with
the original conflict itself. The *real* problem in this family is
not Christie's school behavior—it's the conflict over
whether or not the whole family is going to have to move.
And, in fact, the disagreement over whether or not the
family is going to move is itself only the tip of the iceberg,
for behind this conflict lie some serious and long-standing
problems *between the parents*. The most important of these
is that John is assuming that Andrea is the same person she
was five years ago, and that she wants the same things from
him and the marriage that she wanted in the past. But
Andrea is *not* the same person. She now has different
expectations and different wants.

It isn't hard to see why John and Andrea chose to
focus on Christie rather than the issues that exist between
the two of them. These are difficult issues to deal with, and
they are full of risk for each parent, so from their point of
view it is easier to deal with Christie. This gives them a
way out of having to face and resolve the changes that
have taken place in their marriage. In other words, Christie
is a diversion. Her school behavior is something they can
agree on and, for the time being, it allows them to forget
about the issues that are dividing them.

Unfortunately, however, this approach won't work; it
almost never does. No matter how much John and Andrea
pull together to try to solve Christie's problems, their own
problems will not go away and will almost certainly surface
at some other time in the marriage. Meanwhile, Christie
will continue to have problems.

These parents need to take some time and bring each

other up to date on what each expects from the other and from the marriage. They may need to work on differences between them that have been hidden throughout the entire marriage. These are not easy things to do, and parents who face this task sometimes need the help of a professional counselor.

My intention here has not been to portray Christie's parents as "bad guys" who are deliberately or consciously picking on their daughter. The worst that can be said about them is that they are acting in a very human way in their attempt to find an easy out. I hope that this case clearly illustrates one way in which a family in conflict can produce a "problem child." There are many variations on this theme, of course, but the underlying dynamics are usually the same or similar.

Sometimes parents who are angry or upset with each other will use their children to express this for them rather than expressing it themselves. An example of this occurs when one parent contradicts messages given to a child by the other parent. For instance, one parent may say that it's okay for their six-year-old to go out and play, and the other parent will counter by saying it's not. Or one parent will maintain that it's okay for a daughter to act like a tomboy while the other parent will encourage her to be a proper "little lady."

Some parents seem to use their children as go-betweens to carry angry feelings between each other. In a situation like this, a child becomes a sort of rope that the parents are using in their own personal tug-of-war, being pulled this way and that as each new conflict arises.

Regardless of the variation, though, the theme is always the same: A "problem child" is a child who is reacting to the conflicts within his or her family, specifically those between the parents.

If you have such a child, you have some work to do. You need to begin to resolve the conflicts between you and your partner. This will not be easy, especially when the conflicts are long-standing ones. It's also important that you do not see *yourself* as "the problem." Blaming yourself or being too critical of yourself will only hinder the work you need to do. Seeing yourself as the problem is just as damaging as seeing someone else as the problem.

VII. HOLDING FAMILY CONFERENCES

In order for families to be healthy places in which to live and grow, family members must communicate with each other. Family members need to feel that the family environment is a safe place in which they can really *share* themselves. They need to share their hurts, frustrations, and disappointments. They need to share their triumphs and victories. They need to feel that it is safe to ask for help and support. They need to feel that criticism will be given fairly and that they in turn will have the chance to offer constructive criticism when appropriate. Family members need to feel that the family is a place where they will be *heard*.

The family conference is an excellent forum in which to develop a healthy family. If handled correctly, the family conference is a low-risk way for family members to try new ways of relating. This in turn can bring about a level of intimacy that may not have existed before. The family conference can also help mold behavior; the new ways of relating and the new skills learned will almost invariably spill over into other areas of family life.

There is nothing mysterious about the idea of a family conference, and many families already have some arrangement which at least approaches this idea. Quite often dinnertime is a kind of family conference at which time people come together to eat and bring each other up to date on what each has been doing. Sometimes the family uses this time to make plans or even solve problems. The difficulty with these kinds of meetings is that they tend to be too informal. In general, family conferences are most productive when they have a certain structure and follow certain rules.

Families who use conferences do so in a variety of

ways. Some use them almost exclusively for problem-solving or conflict resolution. There is nothing inherently wrong with this, provided that a conflict does not escalate into a crisis before people get around to talking about it. Crises in a family *can* be dealt with in a family conference setting, but this can be a tricky situation. When conflicts build into crises, people's feelings are usually very intense, and it may be necessary for family members to spend a good deal of time cooling down before they can begin to communicate in a rational way.

One way to avoid the crisis approach is by having *regular* family conferences. In fact, it is wise to schedule one every week *whether or not a problem or conflict exists*. Families who do this find that they have *fewer* crises than before because they can deal with problems when they first appear.

Another benefit of the regular conference is that it offers family members the opportunity to share things that have nothing to do with conflict resolution or problem-solving and which may get pushed out of the way otherwise. I am talking about things like the hopes and dreams that families have, the hopes and dreams that *individual* family members have, and the minor frustrations that each person experiences as he or she goes out into the world. These may seem insignificant when compared to some things that go on in families, but it's a nice feeling to be able to share them with the people you live with and love.

If you find that regular conferences will not work for your family, it's still possible to have successful intermittent ones. In these cases, of course, the question is always one of *when*. Other than not letting things get out of hand before you get together and talk, a good rule of thumb is to hold a conference if something is currently happening, has happened, or is about to happen that affects everyone in the family. Such events might include any major change in the family, such as a relocation; changes in the family structure, such as divorce, remarriage, etc.; something that has happened to one family member that requires the support of other family members; or conflicts or disagreements that are serious enough to affect everyone.

Many issues can be the subjects of family conferences, including some very personal ones. When families talk about the advisability of holding conferences, the question of privacy often comes up. People want to know if they are supposed to reveal *everything* in a conference. What about personal issues between husband and wife? Do parents have to tell their kids everything? And do kids have to tell their parents everything?

It's difficult to give a precise answer to this question because families have different feelings about the sharing of intimate information. In some families there are almost no limits as to what can and cannot be discussed; other families impose many limits. The family conference can work in both kinds of families.

My own feeling is that most families do not share enough of the truly personal, and this book is, in part, an attempt to remedy this by showing you how to have the kind of family in which people will feel safe enough to share their deepest concerns. Even in a family that has attained this ideal, however, not everything has to be shared.

This does not mean that some issues absolutely cannot be talked about, though. The problem, then, is how to share personal information while at the same time maintaining some privacy.

TO TELL OR NOT TO TELL: A CASE STUDY

A couple decided to start seeing a marriage counselor. They were both in their forties, had been married for twelve years, and had two children—a boy, ten years old, and a girl, eight years old.

This couple had recently begun to have some serious disagreements. Each felt that sex was the issue. Things had reached a point where they were not sleeping together; the wife was sleeping in the bedroom and the husband in the guest room.

Although there were many problems between the husband and wife, the one that seemed the most troublesome was the question of what they were supposed to tell their children. Both children had asked why Daddy was sleeping in the guest room and, although the parents wanted to be honest with their children, they were embarrassed to discuss their sexual conflicts. And so they said nothing.

The counselor suggested that they could talk with their children about the conflicts they were having *without talking about sex*. He maintained that the sexual aspect of their conflict was *between them* and should remain there. Furthermore, there was nothing to be gained by talking about sex; the children were too young to understand, and they almost certainly wouldn't care. What concerned the children were other aspects of the conflict. Were the parents going to get a divorce? Were the parents angry at *them?*

The couple returned to the counselor a week later and reported that everything had gone well. The whole family had gotten together one evening to talk about what was happening. The parents had been open and honest about the fact that they were having some disagreements. The children had had some concerns and the parents had listened carefully to them. Not once had the subject of sex come up; it really *hadn't* been necessary to discuss it.

This same approach can be taken with other kinds of sensitive material. In other words, you can share a great deal in a family conference without having to share everything. It's a general rule that when something is going on with one or two members of a family, the other family members will not really be concerned with *all* the details. What they will usually want to know is how it will affect the relationships in the family and, more specifically, how it will affect *them*. These things can usually be talked about without having to reveal everything.

With one or two exceptions, the protection of privacy

should also extend to children and adolescents. They need privacy as much as adults do. The only exceptions are times when a child's immediate physical or emotional health is in jeopardy. Let's look at a couple of examples.

Your twelve-year-old daughter comes home and tells you that as she was walking home from school a man grabbed her and tried to take off her clothes. But when you try to find out the details, she refuses to talk, saying only that it's too embarrassing. What do you do?

In this case, your child's immediate physical and emotional health may be in jeopardy. In order to take care of her, you need to know *exactly* what happened. Did the man physically injure her? Did he threaten her? Was there any sexual contact? You need to know these things, and you need to know them fairly quickly. If after assuring her that it's safe to tell you all that happened your daughter refuses to talk, you may have to press her for details. In this instance her physical and emotional health are more important than her privacy.

Your eight-year-old son comes home from school crying. He says that some kids are calling him names, but when you ask him to tell you more about it he shakes his head. You talk to his teacher, but she can add nothing to the story. What do you do?

You would like to know just what was said and who said it, so your first impulse might be to sit him down and get him to tell you. But this would not be wise. Of course it's no fun to be called names, but it's not a life-and-death situation. And, since your son's physical and emotional health are *not* in jeopardy, you should respect his privacy.

It may be difficult for you to accept the fact that the younger members of your family also have the right to privacy. As parents, you have a tremendous responsibility to care for your children, and in order to care for them you need to know what is going on with them. But before you pressure them for details they may not be ready to talk

about, stop and ask yourself if you *really* need to know
everything. Can you leave them some private space? Truly
wise and caring parents know when to stop. Like adults,
children sometimes need to disclose themselves in their own
time and in their own way. Provided you give them a clear
message that you want to know what is going on with
them and that you are there to listen whenever they want
to talk, your children will almost certainly confide in you
without your having to force them to do so.

I want to turn now to the more general issue of how
to conduct successful family conferences. First, as the name
implies, a family conference should be a *family* affair. This
means that everyone in the family should be included.
Even very young children are interested in and can
contribute to such gatherings. You may want to make an
exception if you're planning to discuss something that you
feel would not be appropriate for very young children,
although in my experience this does not happen very often.

It's best if conferences are held during quiet and
relaxed times. This means setting aside some time when
nothing else is going on in your family. Try to schedule
your conferences so that family members don't have to
juggle their own activities in order to attend them. This can
be difficult, but with a little imagination and persistence it
can usually be done. Incidentally, meal times are *not* the
best settings for conferences—there is usually too much
going on during meals for people to be able to concentrate
on other issues.

Try to set a time limit for your meetings. Forty-five
minutes to an hour works for most families. Having a time
limit is important because most children (and many adults)
have difficulty paying attention for more than forty-five
minutes or an hour. If your children are younger than
seven or eight years old, you might want to set a shorter
limit.

Having a time limit does not mean that you need to
watch the clock and stop precisely when your time is up. If

someone is in the middle of something, give him or her time to finish. But if it looks as if there is still a lot more that needs to be discussed, it's usually better to schedule another conference than it is to push ahead.

It's neither necessary nor wise to have one person act as the facilitator in family conferences, since this sets him or her apart from the rest of the group. It is difficult and confusing to be a facilitator *and* a member of the group at the same time because of the two separate roles involved. This doesn't mean that conferences don't need some facilitating—only that it should be *everyone's* job to see that the rules are followed and to help other people if they are having difficulty expressing themselves.

Think of the first few meetings as experiments. After all, this is a new learning experience for your family. Your first meetings may not be very successful because it's difficult and sometimes frustrating to learn new ways of communicating and you may find yourself slipping back into old patterns. Give yourself and others permission to try new things and make mistakes.

You may also want to set aside the first one or two meetings just to talk about this new experience. Discuss the rules and find out where people might have problems. Explore what it feels like to try something new. And, since most people will be somewhat nervous in the beginning, try to get everyone to share their nervousness and anxiety.

The primary goal of your family conferences should be to increase the intimacy within your family. This may mean discarding or revising some old parent-child and parent-parent relationships. Talk about what you think this will mean to you. For instance, your children may want the freedom to criticize you. Are you ready for this? Do you have enough self-confidence to allow your children to give you negative feedback? Or are you afraid that this will undermine your authority? Younger family members will have their own concerns about this issue, and they should be encouraged to share these, too.

After one or two meetings, when you feel ready to discuss an issue, pick something that is *nonthreatening.* Don't start off trying to solve some long-standing family conflict; leave topics like these for later, when you all feel more secure about this new way of relating. You might start off by talking about how to make your family a better place to live and letting everyone contribute ideas. Or take a poll and find out if someone needs special help with something. Never mind that what you are talking about may seem trivial compared to other things that are happening in your family. It's better to start slowly and let everyone have the experience of what it feels like to relate in new and healthier ways.

There are only a few rules that need to be followed in the family conference setting, but they are important. You might even want to write them down and post them before each meeting so there are no misunderstandings.

The following are offered as guidelines. In time, you'll undoubtedly want to add to this list to suit your own family's style and needs.

1. *No one should be forced to say anything he or she doesn't want to say.* This means that putting pressure on other people who indicate that they don't want to discuss a particular subject is unacceptable.

2. *Everyone who wants to say something should have the chance.* This can be divided into two rules: (a) no one should interrupt while another is speaking, and (b) no one should be allowed to monopolize the meeting. If someone does try to monopolize the meeting, he or she should be stopped. These may seem like contradictory rules, but they are not. People who try to monopolize meetings are not really adding anything to them. Instead, they are trying to control them, either because they want to prevent something from happening or to avoid discussing a certain issue. This is the same as filibustering, and it should always be stopped.

3. *No one should be allowed to injure anyone else.* The

obvious interpretation of this rule is that no one should be permitted to do physical harm to any other family member. But sometimes words can hurt as much as physical blows, so it also means that no one should be allowed to embarrass or belittle anyone else—even during times when emotions are running high. If people get angry or feel as if they are being hurt, it's okay to express these emotions honestly and directly, but these expressions should never turn into attacks or opportunities for revenge.

The overall goals of family life are to have the kind of family in which people can trust one another, feel safe enough to share their intimate concerns, and be supportive of one another. Although it's everyone's responsibility to help build this kind of family structure, parents in particular have a special role.

Ideally, everyone will be equal in most family conferences. Each person's thoughts and feelings will have equal validity and carry equal weight. Sometimes, though, you as an adult will have to act as the final authority. But even when this is true you should still avoid "pulling rank."

For instance, let's say that you feel the need to have some more help around the house. You gather everyone together and announce, "From now on everyone has to help with the chores. Any questions?" This is *not* a family conference, it's more like a memo to your employees. Even when you have the final say, as in the case of limits and rules, you can almost always allow for discussion. Begin with a statement of your own thoughts and feelings and then encourage others to share theirs.

One technique that aids effective communication is the use of I-messages. An I-message is a way for you to take responsibility for whatever you are saying or feeling. It also lets everyone know exactly what is going on with you— what you want or don't want, what you like or dislike. Let's look at an example.

One of the goals in your family is for everyone to be home for dinner. Lately, though, this has not been happening, so you all decide to hold a conference to discuss this issue. As you listen to other people talk, you start realizing that you have some strong feelings on the subject. Now it's your turn. How do you communicate your strong feelings?

Here are some options:

I-Message: "I would like to have everyone home for dinner. It's very important to me."

No I-Message: "You know, it's nice to have everyone home for dinner. I mean, families should have at least *one* meal together, don't you think?"

The first option—the I-message—is a clear statement of what you want. The second is much less clear and direct, so it's hard for others to learn from it what you really want. If people aren't sure what you want, the whole issue is likely to remain fuzzy. So say what *you* want, what *you* feel, and what *you* think.

It may seem fairly simple to start using I-messages, but in fact it can be difficult, especially when you're not sure of what you're thinking or feeling, or when you feel that others don't really want to know what you're thinking or feeling. Even people who are in the habit of using I-messages are likely to slip back into less direct ways of expressing themselves from time to time. When this happens, it's sometimes helpful if someone points it out. If a member of your family is expressing something in an indirect way, you might try asking her or him to use an I-message. But be sure to do so in a supportive and helpful way.

Another good habit to get into is that of checking out your own assumptions about the other people in your family. It's never safe to assume that you know what others are thinking or feeling; wrong assumptions can lead to ineffective communication and confusion. Actually, assumptions work in two ways: *You* can assume things about others, and others can assume things about *you*. If everyone examined their assumptions about *other* people there would be no need to go any further with this, but unfortunately this doesn't always happen. So in addition to checking out your assumptions about others, it's sometimes necessary to check out *their* assumptions about *you*.

Let's look at an example which illustrates the importance of checking out assumptions.

> You and your daughter have been disagreeing about how late she should be allowed to stay out on school nights. One day after school, you ask her to sit down with you and talk. After you say what you think, you ask her to tell you what she thinks. She frowns. What do you do?

At this point, you have two options. You can make assumptions about what your daughter is feeling and act on them, or you can examine your assumptions. Here are the probable consequences of each in turn:

> Option 1: You assume that because she is frowning she doesn't agree with what you have just said and doesn't even want to talk about it. So you begin feeling defensive. Your daughter senses your defensiveness and bristles in return—and off you go, right into an argument.

> Option 2: You ask your daughter what her frown means or what she is feeling while she is frowning. She says that while she would like to talk about how late she should be allowed to stay out on school nights, she would rather do this at some other time. Right now she's supposed to be at the house of a friend she promised to visit. She was frowning because she didn't know how to tell you that she didn't feel like talking just then. You listen to her and agree that some other time would be okay. By finding out what your daughter was really feeling, you've saved both of you from an unpleasant and unnecessary scene.

Effective listening is perhaps the most important technique in communication and the most difficult to learn. Real listening is an art and a skill. It's the ability to turn off whatever is going on inside your own head and really *hear* what another person is saying. This isn't easy, and it's *not* the same as just listening to the *words* the other person is saying. It means that, at that particular moment, you devote your full and complete attention to the other person. You listen because you want to *know* what the other is saying. This takes practice.

As you become more aware of how you and others listen, you will begin to notice that most of the time people listen to others as a kind of courtesy. If we don't listen to *them*, they won't listen to *us*. And most of the time people already have their minds made up about what they are going to say next, even before another person is finished talking. Practice your listening skills and you'll begin to really *understand* what others are trying to say to you.

If you would like more information on communications skills, there are several good books on the subject. But at some point you will have to stop your reading and put into practice what you have learned, and things will almost certainly not go the way they are "supposed to" according to the books.

Remember that the family conference is an *experiment* you and your family are undertaking together. Give yourself credit for trying this experiment, and give yourself permission to make mistakes.

VIII. RECOGNIZING SHADOWS

Any unresolved conflicts you have as an individual will probably become issues as you live your role as a parent. For instance, if you are the kind of person who backs away from conflict, you may have difficulty being firm about the limits you set for your children's behavior. These personal conflicts become important in parenting because parents often tend to *externalize* them onto their children. The way this usually works is that a child acts out one side or part of a conflict his or her parent is going through. And this can cause a great many problems.

Almost every child takes after one or both parents. If you like to watch movies, your children will probably like to watch movies too. If you are a quiet person, one or more of your children is likely to have similar characteristics. But there are less obvious similarities between parents and children. What about those characteristics which your children have taken from you and now display, characteristics you're not even aware you have? Perhaps they are things about yourself you have forgotten, or conflicts you have pushed out of your conscious mind.

You are probably aware of the stereotyped "pushy parents" who goad their children to excel in certain activities; this happens quite often in sports. These parents are often trying to make up for something missing in their own lives, and they use their children to do this. Of course they are almost always unaware of their real motives, and they are quite sincere when they say that they are doing something "for the good of the child." To an outsider, however, it doesn't seem as if the child is benefiting at all; in fact, he or she may seem unhappy and maladjusted.

It is normal to have expectations for your children, to

want them to be a certain way, or to want certain things for them. You may want them to be happy and to have a satisfying life; perhaps you want them to get more out of life than you did. You may want your son or daughter to become a teacher, a scientist, or an artist—the possibilities are endless. As with most things in life, this particular aspect of parenting is a problem only when *it's carried to an extreme.* Let's look at two case studies to see how this works.

THE POPULAR SISTERS: A CASE STUDY

Teresa Silverman was a single parent with two children— Gayle, thirteen and Danielle, fourteen. In all respects but one theirs was a happy, close-knit family. The exception was the subject of dating.

Teresa and her daughters argued endlessly about whether or not the girls were old enough to date. The girls said they were, the mother said they weren't. Sometimes during these arguments Teresa felt so disheartened that she even regretted having taken custody of her daughters.

To make matters worse, Gayle and Danielle were very popular. They were popular with classmates of both sexes, but especially with the boys. Sometimes it seemed to Teresa that her daughters were in love with half the boys in school—and the other half were in love with them. There were always boys hanging around the house or calling on the phone.

Teresa knew that other parents experienced the same problems with their children, but that didn't make her feel any better. She also knew that "things were different these days," and that even eighth and ninth graders "went steady." But that didn't help either. She wondered if she was—as her daughters had hinted—a little old-fashioned and out of step with the times on this issue.

Teresa was good at setting limits on her daughters' behavior in other areas, but not on the "boy" issue. All her attempts failed until finally she stopped trying. But this didn't end the conflict, and each new boyfriend became the occasion for a bitter argument.

Teresa had been divorced for six years; she rarely saw her ex-husband Bob, although the girls spent a considerable amount of time with him. Bob was the only man she had ever been seriously involved with. They had married right out of high school, and Teresa mentally kicked herself whenever she thought about how young she had been— much too young to have gotten married.

Although many men were interested in her now, Teresa preferred to keep her relationships casual. She preferred to devote her time and energy to her job and her two children.

The arguments between Teresa and her daughters finally became so serious that Teresa decided to seek professional counseling. After about a month the counselor pointed out that sometimes Teresa sounded jealous when she talked about her daughters and their boyfriends. At first Teresa denied this. After all, she was an attractive woman and could have all the men she wanted, so why should she be jealous of her own daughters?

Then the counselor asked Teresa to talk about her own childhood, and especially how boys had fit into the picture. Teresa related how her mother had been very strict about boys, much stricter than she was with her own children. Teresa had not been alone with a boy until she was sixteen years old. She remembered being thirteen years old and feeling cheated by her mother's strictness. She remembered daydreaming about going to movies and parties like the rest of her friends were allowed to do.

But there was more to it than that. Even though Teresa hadn't liked her mother's rules about boys, she believed that her mother had basically been right. She had believed it when she was thirteen, and *she still did.*

In the counseling sessions that followed, Teresa learned more about her conflict. She discovered that she wanted some kind of intimate relationship with a man—not marriage, perhaps, but something more committed than she now had. But every time she started to get serious about a man she could hear her mother's voice saying that *she had better things to do.*

COMMENTS ON THE CASE STUDY

When parents externalize their conflicts onto their children, the children often act out one side or another. In this case, Teresa's conflict concerned men. On the one hand she wanted a more intimate relationship; on the other hand, she didn't. As in all conflicts, both a *yes* and a *no* existed.

Gayle and Danielle were acting out the *yes* side of Teresa's conflict; by having plenty of boys in their life. One way of looking at this is by seeing that Teresa's daughters were doing exactly what Teresa herself had wanted to do when she was their age. But while she had only yearned and daydreamed about having fun and having boyfriends, her daughters were actually doing these things.

It's not enough to say that the girls were passively acting out part of Teresa's conflict because in one sense Teresa was encouraging them. She was giving them mixed messages—both a yes and a no. Her words said NO!, but her actions said YES! In order to see the YES! message, it is important to remember that she was jealous of her daughters' success with boys and that she was not able to set limits on their behavior. In these ways, indirect as they might seem, she was telling her daughters what they were doing was okay. She was giving her approval.

But a problem arose between Teresa and her daughters because every time Gayle or Danielle announced a new boyfriend, it touched off the conflict within Teresa about her own attitudes toward men. She could not accept in her daughters what she could not accept in herself. And so the arguments and the fights began.

Teresa stayed in counseling, and she began to resolve

her conflict about men. Once she admitted that it was *her* conflict, she relaxed, and her attitude toward her daughters changed. She became less critical, and not surprisingly, the arguments stopped.

THE CONCERNED PARENT: A CASE STUDY

Like Teresa Silverman, Ruth Simpson was also a single parent. Her son Marcus had just started the fifth grade. Ruth was a concerned and involved parent, active in the PTA and always the first to volunteer for committees and fund-raising events.

Marcus was a successful student. In fact, he was usually his teacher's favorite. He worked hard and almost always got straight A's. But things started changing almost as soon as he began the fifth grade. Marcus became interested in sports, and he didn't put as much effort into his school work as he had before. As a result, his grades slipped a little.

Mrs. Brown, Marcus's fifth-grade teacher, wasn't particularly worried. An experienced teacher, she knew that things like this were normal. And anyway, she thought as she made out the year's first report card, Marcus was still a B+ student and could be a straight-A-student any time he wanted. Mrs. Brown was not prepared for what happened next.

The report cards went out at 3:00 P.M. on Friday. At 3:45 P.M. Mrs. Brown received a call from Ruth Simpson; Marcus's mother sounded so upset that at first Mrs. Brown thought something had happened to Marcus.

But it wasn't that at all. Mrs. Simpson was upset about her son's report card and she wanted a conference. Mrs. Brown agreed to schedule one. During the conference, Ruth Simpson spent the entire time emphasizing how important it was that Marcus's grades improve. She said that she would do anything Mrs. Brown suggested.

Although Mrs. Brown reassured her that everything

was fine and that Marcus was still a superior student, Ruth Simpson wouldn't listen. Finally, Mrs. Brown realized that something else was involved, and she suggested that Marcus's mother talk with the school psychologist.

And this was the story Ruth Simpson told to the school psychologist: She had had a difficult life. Both of her parents were semi-invalids, and by the time she was fifteen Ruth was practically supporting the family. Although she finished high school, which took an extraordinary amount of work on her part, she didn't have the chance to go on to college. Now it was too late—too late for college and too late, she felt, for her to get the things she wanted from life.

But it was not too late for her son. Marcus could have everything he wanted, everything Ruth had always wanted for herself, and Ruth was determined to see that he got it. That's why it was so important for him to do well in school.

The school psychologist had no luck getting Ruth to relax. Nor did she have any success getting her to see the connection between her *own* unfulfilled dreams and the pressure she was putting on Marcus.

The rest of the school year was hell for Marcus and his mother as well as Mrs. Brown. Marcus's grades continued to slip ever so slightly, and at each slip his mother pressured him to improve. By the end of the fifth grade Marcus was a B student—and he hated school.

****

Although the above two case studies are different, the principle is the same: in each case the children became the expression of their parents' conflicts. The parents externalized their own conflicts onto their children.

How can you tell if something like this is happening in your family? And if it is, what can you do about it?

The first step is to forget about the conflicts between you and your children. Instead, take some time and concentrate on yourself. Specifically, you need to take yourself back to your childhood and recall what growing up was like for you.

If you answered the questions at the end of the first chapter, get out your answers now. Make any additions or deletions you wish.

What was it like for you as a child? What were *you* like? What dreams and wishes did you have? Were you, like Teresa, kept under strict supervision? And did you, as she did, dream of being free to enjoy yourself?

What were you like as a teenager? Were you quiet? Noisy? Did you get into much trouble? How did you get along with members of the opposite sex? What did you think about school?

Continue reading through the questions and your answers. Take some time with this. And remember, it's *your* memories that count. If you remember yourself as being a quiet child but your parents say you were noisy, it's the way *you* remember things that's important.

It may help to look back at photographs taken of you as a child and a teenager. Find as many as you can.

The next step in this self-examination process is to bring yourself back to the present. How are you now compared to the way you were as a child? How have you changed? Again, take your time with these questions. Don't worry if you feel you haven't remembered everything, or if there are some things you don't want to think about now. Sometimes it's difficult to get in touch with these parts of yourself, especially if you still have conflicts about them.

Now think about the conflicts that exist between you and your children, especially those that never seem to end. What are you in conflict about? School performance? Piano lessons? Their friends?

Finally, put all of this information together. Do you see any connections between the issues that concerned you when you were younger (and maybe still do) and the areas of conflict between you and your children? The answers may not come right away, and you may change your mind several times, but keep asking these questions and looking for answers. The longer you are willing to stay with it, the more you will learn.

Remember that it's normal to have expectations. Problems arise when the expectations you have for *your children* are really expectations you had and still have for yourself.

If you have identified one or two areas where you are externalizing your conflicts onto your children, it is essential that you reclaim each conflict as your own. In the first case study in this chapter, Teresa had to reclaim the conflict she had about men. She had to acknowledge it as her *own* before the conflict between her and her daughters could be resolved. The same was true of Ruth Simpson; before she could relax about her son and stop putting undue pressure on him, she had to realize that she still had unresolved fears and hopes about herself. After you have reclaimed that lost or forgotten part of yourself, you can then decide what you want to do about it. You may want to start resolving the part of the conflict that is still with you, or you may not; that choice is up to you. If you want to *completely* resolve these kinds of parent-child conflicts, you will probably have to work out your own conflicts first. But whether or not you choose to do this, it is *very* important that you at least take responsibility for your own conflicts and acknowledge them as *yours*. This act on your part will almost certainly help any parent-child conflicts you are experiencing, for by accepting your conflicts as your own you will be putting some distance between you and your children. You will be separating your life and your concerns from their lives and their concerns, and you will be able to see each more clearly in the future.

IX. GREAT EXPECTATIONS

Just as the expectations that parents have of their children can sometimes lead to parent-child conflicts, the things parents expect from each other can also lead to conflicts.

This issue seems to be at the root of many family difficulties. Almost every couple who comes to me for counseling must sooner or later work on the expectations each partner has of the other—expectations which, most of the time, have never been openly expressed.

WHAT THEY REALLY WANTED: A CASE STUDY

Nancy and Don were in their mid-twenties. Nancy worked as a receptionist, and Don drove a delivery truck for a local bakery. They hadn't known each other long before they got married, and the marriage surprised most of their friends. It was clearly a case of "opposites attract."

Nancy was the mover and the doer. She always seemed to be working on some project. She was also taking classes in computer programming, knowing that she wouldn't be happy being a receptionist for the rest of her life.

Don, on the other hand, seemed to take things easy. He liked his job. If something better came along he would take it, but he wasn't going to spend a lot of energy looking. He was also content to let Nancy handle the household finances and most of the other family business.

The first year of their marriage went well; the second didn't. In fact, during the second year the bottom seemed to fall out and they fought constantly. Neither could point to anything specific, so the fighting was confusing. They had had their share of arguments during the first year, and it did bother them that they weren't able to settle these arguments, but they never lasted long and were soon forgotten. Now, however, the arguments were real fights that lasted for days. Both Nancy and Don hoped that this was just a phase that would end soon.

But it didn't end, and things got progressively worse. Nancy's migraines, which hadn't bothered her in years, returned. And while in the past Don could hardly wait to get home after work, he now began staying out late and drinking with his friends.

****

In order to understand what was happening to this couple, we first need to look at the kind of family each person came from and see how each of them developed certain expectations about a marriage partner.

Nancy's mother divorced her husband when Nancy was five years old. When Nancy was eleven her mother was stricken with an incapacitating disease, and for the next few years Nancy divided her time between going to school and taking care of her invalid mother and her two younger brothers.

Nancy's relatives lavished praise on her for being so capable and so responsible at such an early age. As she grew up, Nancy believed that *her best quality was her ability to take care of any situation and do it well.* But secretly—so secretly that she didn't even admit it to herself—she longed for a time when she could stop taking care of other people and someone would take care of her. She knew that it would happen some day. She *expected* it to happen.

When she met Don, she realized that he was a man who would let her continue in her accustomed role of the person who "took care of things." She also admired his ability to relax and take things easy and, in a vague way, hoped that some of this would rub off on her. But Nancy had a stronger hope and a stronger expectation. She *expected* that Don would take charge of the relationship, would take charge of *her*, would tell her to stop and relax; in other words, that he would take care of her. She never told him this. She wasn't even aware that this was what she expected, but she expected it nevertheless.

Don's parents were never divorced, although they might as well have been. They fought constantly and the family was always in a state of turmoil.

Don liked both of his parents, although to his youthful eye his mother seemed the stronger of the two. He was his mother's favorite in turn, and she took him into her confidence. She never seemed to tire of telling him how disappointed she was in his father and how his father would never amount to much unless she kept after him.

As he grew up, Don developed into an easy-going sort of person, so easy-going that to the outside world he seemed to have no ambition. But Don had lots of dreams. He dreamed of owning his own business, although he wasn't sure what that would be. He never told anyone of these dreams, not even his closest friends; he seldom even admitted them to himself. He also had the vague feeling that he wouldn't make it on his own and that he needed someone to push him.

In Nancy he saw a person of enormous energy and determination and he respected her for this. In a vague way he thought that maybe she could teach him to be more forceful or, better yet, that she would take him under her wing and give him a little shove. He expected that someday she would do this, although he never told her of this expectation.

****

Let's stop for a moment and see what we have here. There are many ways of describing Don and Nancy's marriage. One way is to say that these two people met and married and expected that the other person would do certain things for them. Don hoped and expected that Nancy would push him along a little, that she would give him some of the energy he lacked. Nancy expected that Don would take over most of the responsibility and tell her that she could relax, that she didn't have to work so hard. *But neither of them ever said a word about what they wanted and expected from the other.* And not only did Don and Nancy expect that the other person would do certain things for them, both believed that *they couldn't do these things for themselves.* Don felt that he couldn't make it without a shove from Nancy, and Nancy felt that she couldn't relax unless Don told her to. Each person wanted to change, to be different, but both felt powerless to make the changes on their own.

It's not surprising that this couple fought. They wanted things from each other, but they didn't say what those things were. And they were disappointed, even angry, when their unvoiced expectations weren't met.

This couple is not unique. We all have expectations of the people we live with, and much of the time we don't say what we're expecting. Indeed, much of the time we are not fully aware that we have certain expectations, and this causes problems. For as long as expectations are kept at a low level of awareness they are potential trouble spots.

The expectation that someone will do something for you that you feel you can't do for yourself is the one that usually causes the most problems in a relationship. It's very hard to uncover and, once uncovered, it points the way to significant changes that need to be made.

How can you tell if something like this is happening in your relationship? One way is to sit down with your partner and talk about your expectations and what they mean. This takes a great deal of trust and honesty, but it can be effective. The only problem is that these expectations can lead to conflict. If this happens, the lines of communication may break, at least for the time being, and the necessary trust and willingness to talk will not be there. Then your only alternative is to take some time and do some work on yourself.

It's important that you start on *yourself*. Many people are tempted to try to figure out their partners rather than work on themselves. That's understandable; it's more fun and less threatening to analyze someone else. But it will be far more valuable in the long run if you concentrate on yourself.

You may find it helpful if you write down some of your thoughts along the way. Simply jot down the expectations you have of your partner. Don't worry about being selective at this point; just write whatever comes to mind. If you're at a loss and you're staring at a blank piece of paper, try using these suggestions:

Lean back and daydream about your partner. Relax and imagine what it would be like if you had a magic wand and could instantly transform your partner into anything you wanted. What would he or she be like? How would he or she be different? Perhaps you would like him or her to be more aggressive. Or less aggressive. Or more tender and loving.

Now think back to the time when you first met your partner. What qualities *really* attracted you to him or her? Was *she* sexy and alluring? Was *he* sexy and alluring? Did he have a lot of friends? Was she a positive thinker? Did he seem to be a happy person?

If these exercises don't work for you and you still end up with nothing on your paper, try to determine why you are holding yourself back—because that is exactly what you're doing. Do you feel this is all childish and stupid and that maybe *you* are childish for going along with it? Do you feel that it would be unrealistic or unreasonable for you to want certain things from your partner or want him or her to change in certain ways? Do you feel that you don't deserve the things you want? Whatever the reason for your hesitation, try to put it aside for now. If you want to make these kinds of judgments, you can do so later. Once you know what your objections are and are able to put them on the shelf, go back through the exercises again.

When you have finished writing, you should have a list of qualities or personality characteristics that describe your partner—those you would like him or her to have, and those you admired in him or her when you were first getting to know each other. If you are like most people, though, what you will *really* have is a list of *expectations* you have of your partner.

Look closely at these expectations. What can they tell you? You may be a bit confused at this stage, so I'll give you some hints. Your expectations can tell you three things:

1. that there is some kind of person you want to be or some specific quality you'd like to have;

2. that it doesn't seem to you as if you can be this person or have this quality through your own efforts; and

3. that you are looking to others (in this case your partner) to give you what you want.

You may be looking to others to supply what you feel is missing from your life, and you are probably not even aware that this is what you are doing.

Is there anything on your list that fits this description? What you're looking for is something you see or admire or want in your partner which in reality you would like to be or have yourself. If nothing on your list seems to fit, don't worry; sometimes it takes time to arrive at these insights.

Expectations are difficult to identify because they usually originate in your childhood and indicate areas in your life where you may need to make some changes. Let's add more information to our case study to see how these ideas apply to the situation Nancy found herself in.

****

Nancy remembered what it was like to be eleven. She remembered how unfair it had seemed that she should have to take care of her family at such an early age. She remembered having a vague wish that someone, some adult, would tell her that she could stop taking care of everyone and go out and play just like all of the other eleven-year-olds she knew. But that never happened, and she soon forgot that she even expected it to happen. But the expectation was there, whether or not it was in her conscious mind.

Nancy also realized how her expectations were putting unspoken demands on Don. When she understod what she was doing, she felt relieved. For most of her life she had been waiting for someone to come along and tell her she could relax, and now she didn't have to do that anymore. She no longer had to place those demands on other people. She realized that *she* was the only person who could give herself permission to relax and, although she didn't yet know how to do this, she nevertheless felt stronger because she now felt that her life was in her own hands.

****

How does this relate to you? Just as Nancy did, you must reclaim your expectations as your own. They are yours. They are a part of you. By reclaiming your expectations, you will begin to stop believing that someone else will make changes for you or in some way make you a different person. If you want things to be different in your life, you are really the only one who can make it happen.

Reclaiming your expectations will also indicate the changes you may need to make. Making such changes involves two processes: a *letting go* of the expectation that someone else will make changes for you, and a *going forward* to develop a new part of your personality.

It's the first process—the letting go—that seems to be the most difficult for many people. Often it gets tied up with deep childhood hurts or frustrations. Perhaps your mother or father didn't give you the love and security you needed; as a child you expected they would, but they didn't. As you grew up, you transferred this expectation to other significant adults in your life, although you were probably not aware of doing this. You may have even chosen your partners because they reminded you of your parents. It's as if you are saying, "Even though I am an adult, I still want and need things my parents never gave me. If I can't get those things from them, I will choose others from whom I *can* get them." This doesn't work, of course, because no one can give you those things—no one but you yourself. So you must learn to give up trying to recreate that old scene. You must let go of your old expectations and move ahead.

Once you have finished with the letting-go process, you will be ready to make the necessary changes in your life. You may encounter even more difficulties during this process. Since you are part of a family system, any major changes you make will affect everyone else in your family. They will especially affect your partner, who may feel threatened and resist your efforts to change. Again, let's use the case of Nancy and Don to illustrate these points.

****

As Nancy began to understand herself better, she decided to share her new awarenesses with Don. At first he didn't understand what she was talking about, but when he did he began to see that Nancy was going to be a different person when this was all over. This was vaguely unsettling to him. Was *he* going to have to change too? It certainly seemed that way.

Don *liked* the fact that Nancy was so energetic and, in a very real way, he was counting on her energy to give him the initiative he felt he couldn't give himself. But now she was saying that she didn't want to be that way anymore. He felt threatened. What was he going to do? How was he going to get along without her support? Because he didn't want Nancy to change, he wasn't very supportive of her efforts. It took him quite a while before he stopped resisting and began to see that there might be some good things in it for him, too.

****

There is risk involved when one partner begins to change. The other partner perceives that things are going to be different and this sometimes comes as a shock and can be experienced, at least at first, as a threat.

The truth is that the other person will *also* have to change. At least, he or she will have to learn to cope with the changes the other person is making. But often there is more to it than that. Often the other partner must make changes in his or her lifestyle or modify old familiar patterns and expectations.

What can you do to minimize the risks and other possibly negative consequences of these kinds of changes? Ideally, you and your partner should undertake changes together. When both partners see the need to change and agree to help each other, they can usually tolerate a certain amount of disruption in their daily lives, at least for a while. This togetherness is the exception, however; it is usually one person who initiates the change, and the other frequently resists it for a time. If you are alone in feeling the need to make changes, I would advise you to relax, go slowly, and appreciate the consequences that your actions will have on your family.

Perhaps you are a woman whose children are grown. You've always expected that your family would be the only important focus of your life, but now you feel the need to be more independent and want to stop relying on others for your sense of self-worth. What should you do? Well, you *should not* suddenly announce that you're chucking it all and going back to school to prepare for a new career! A better approach is to go slowly and do some groundwork.

Get some feedback from your family and find out where problems may arise as you start making the changes you want to make in your life.

The changes you decide on should *not* be dependent on what others say or feel, however. This is important for you to realize. Still, keeping in touch with your family along the way will help them to feel much less threatened. You may even find that you want to make some compromises.

It is also helpful to give your family some reassurance by saying, "I am the one who feels the need to be different, and I am not asking or demanding that anyone else be different." Of course, this isn't entirely true. You probably will want your family to give you some support, or at least to resist the urge to sabotage your efforts. As much as possible, though, communicate to them that the changes you are making are *your* changes. By doing this you will be giving the others in your family some room, and they will have less reason to feel threatened.

In order to develop this attitude, it's important that you see yourself as a person who is separate from the rest of your family. In some ways, of course, your life is bound to theirs, but you are also an individual in your own right. If you aren't comfortable with this, you may fall into the trap of feeling that you cannot make changes unless others also change or actively support you. And if you believe that these are prerequisites for your changing, you may stop yourself and create some unnecessary hostility in those around you.

You *can* make any changes you want to make. It helps if others are supportive, but you don't need anyone's permission to change and you don't *have* to have anyone else's help.

X. COPING WITH ADOLESCENCE

Psychologists and other social scientists love to write about adolescence. There seems to be more written about this age group than any other. And here I am, adding my two cents' worth!

In my experience as a family therapist, this is the age group that parents seem to have the most problems with. It works the other way, too—adolescents seem to have more problems with their parents than children do. But why? Obviously, no one has come up with all of the answers to this question. But I do want to tell you a story about something that happened to me that gave me new insights into the issue.

Several years ago I was working with a group of parents who started talking about teenagers. Several parents had teenagers, and everyone seemed to be having some problems coping with them.

After the session was over, a man and woman came up to me and asked if they could talk to me privately for a few minutes. I had noticed that during the group they had listened intently as other parents told of their experiences. Although this couple had said nothing during the group discussion, it was obvious that they were upset and worried.

As they began talking, I realized that they were more than merely upset and worried. They were *scared*. The father kept saying that he just didn't understand teenagers; they were a complete mystery to him and he didn't know what he was going to do about his own children. The mother voiced her feelings of helplessness, too. As I listened to them, I thought to myself that the teenagers in this family must be involved in something really serious—like drugs, perhaps. Or maybe there was an adolescent daughter who was pregnant.

At one point in our discussion, I asked the couple how old their children were. The mother replied that they had a son who was seven years old and a daughter who was six. I must not have realized what they had just said, because I immediately asked, "And your teenagers, how old are they?"

The mother looked confused by my question. Then she said that they didn't *have* any teenagers. Now *I* was confused! I even asked them if they were *sure* they didn't have teenagers! I must have sounded funny, because they both laughed.

Once we cleared up the confusion, I asked them why they were so worried. After all, their children were still so young! Both parents said the same thing: *They had heard such awful stories about how hard it was to deal with teenagers that they wanted to be ready!* Even though they were not having *any* problems with their children at the moment, these parents were convinced that once their children turned twelve or thirteen their family was going to be a disaster.

And they were not unique in their fears. I have often heard parents of teenagers say to parents of younger children, "Just wait until your kids are as old as ours. If you think you have problems now, just wait!" In this way the myth of the "impossible adolescent" gets passed on from parent to parent.

I feel that this attitude works like a self-fulfilling prophecy: you expect something bad to happen, you get ready for it even before anything has actually happened, and you end up by your tension and apprehension *creating* the very thing you are most afraid of. I am convinced that at least *some* of the problems that exist between teenagers and their parents are due to this phenomenon.

But parents aren't the only ones who are responsible for this prophecy of doom. If you read the literature on adolescence—the books and articles and Sunday supplements—you'll find that it's mostly negative. Although much of it is presented in scholarly language which seems to be objective, what it all boils down to is this: Teenagers are likely to be overemotional, confused, hooked on drugs, and rude to their parents and other adults. They are also likely to get pregnant or to get someone else pregnant, and they will run away from home if you don't do what they want you to do.

Because they are going through rather profound physical and social changes, adolescents do need support and nurturing and safety. Unfortunately, it is at this time of their lives that adolescents also must make the often jarring change from elementary school to junior high school. Making that transition is very difficult for many youngsters.

I once asked a sixth-grade class to talk about their feelings about going into the seventh grade. Almost two-thirds of them expressed anxiety about the change. I have since talked with many sixth-graders about this, and I have always gotten the same or a similar response. And these were, for the most part, normal and well-adjusted kids.

What are they afraid of? Here's a sampling: They're afraid of being "trashed" by the older students. They're afraid of being lost in the hustle and bustle. They're afraid that they won't make new friends and will lose track of the ones they've made in grade school. They're afraid of the drugs and the violence they have heard so much about—and often their fears are substantiated. Given these and other very real anxieties, what can you do?

You can begin by assuming that your children, if they are about to make this change, *will* have anxieties and concerns and will benefit from talking about them. Start encouraging them to do so when they are in the latter part of the sixth grade, as this is the time when most sixth-graders really begin thinking about junior high. Keep in close touch with them throughout the summer, and make a special effort to talk to them a couple of days before school starts. Sit down with them again soon after school starts. Let your children talk about what the experience feels like to them. Although all children can benefit from this kind of attention, it is especially important for children who have relatively undeveloped social skills—that is, those who have difficulties making friends or who are especially shy. These are the kids who really get lost in junior high and they need *special* help.

It is *not* safe to assume that someone at school will notice if your child is starting to have problems and offer to help. If your child needs extra support and encouragement, it will almost certainly have to come from you, because in the average junior high neither the teachers nor the counselors have the time or the energy to give much special attention to their students.

What can you as a parent do to help make adolescence an easier time? First, it does help to *relax* and work on developing the right attitude. Having teenagers *can* be a positive experience; all things considered, coping with adolescents is no more difficult than coping with young children. It *is* different, however, and to be successful you may need to be aware of some of these differences. You may also need to make a couple of changes in the way you play your parenting role.

The issue of how to control children's behavior seems especially critical during adolescence. The following case study illustrates a few of the problems that frequently arise in this area.

SHE'LL DO WHAT SHE WANTS: A CASE STUDY

Pam and Steve's daughter Jessica was in the seventh grade. Although Jessica and her parents had had their share of arguments, none of them had seemed too serious. . .until now. Now it seemed as though they fought all the time. And their fights always revolved around two issues.

The first had to do with clothes. In order to be ready for junior high, mother and daughter had shopped for a new wardrobe for Jessica during the summer. Although Pam had selected most of Jessica's new clothes, this had not seemed to bother Jessica at the time and she had liked what they had bought. But now Jessica claimed that her new clothes made her look like a sixth-grader. She was embarrassed by them and wanted a whole new set.

The other issue centered on whether or not Jessica was to be allowed to stay out later on school nights. As things stood now, she was not allowed to do this. But Jessica insisted that since everyone else stayed out later, why shouldn't she? Besides, how could she make any friends if she had to be home and in bed by 9:30 every night?

Pam and Steve said no to both issues: no new clothes, and no staying out later on school nights. This made Jessica angry. Her parents expected that things would blow over in a couple of days; they always had in the past. But this time they didn't, and the arguments just got worse. It was apparent that Jessica was not going to give in quietly. Pam and Steve soon realized that they were facing an entirely unfamiliar situation and would have to do something about it fast. They also recognized that Jessica's actions were causing *their* feelings to change. They felt threatened because Jessica had never acted like this before. They had the uneasy feeling that sooner or later their daughter was going to do what she wanted, regardless of what *they* wanted. They were also scared that if they gave in on these issues Jessica wouldn't stop there. Sooner or later, they felt, she would be in *real* trouble—she might even get pregnant or start using drugs.

COMMENTS ON THE CASE STUDY

This family's predicament is very typical. As a counselor, I've watched many parents play this same scene or a variation on it.

The one parental feeling that stands out in cases like these is the parents' *fear* that they will no longer be able to control their children's behavior. What happens next, in many instances, is that the parents act out this fear by redoubling their efforts to control their children's behavior. Quite predictably, the children react negatively to the increased control, and a seemingly never-ending succession of fights and arguments begins. This is certainly not the only reason why parents and their adolescent children argue, but I have seen it happen so many times that I consider it a prime cause.

How do families get into this position, and what can they do about it? The answers to these questions revolve around two issues: how much control of your children's behavior is okay, and when you have to start letting go.

When a child is an infant, the parents must take complete responsibility for all aspects of that child's life, which is just another way of saying that they must *control* all aspects of that child's life. Parents who can share some of this responsibility are extremely lucky. Our society generally forces parents to take *all* of the responsibility. Young families break away from *their* families, and they move often, so there are seldom grandparents or other relatives around to take on some of the responsibility. To make matters worse, few communities have affordable and readily available daycare centers. So most parents end up having to do this tremendously difficult job alone. What this all means is that it's often difficult for parents to *let go* of some of the responsibility for—and control over—their children's lives. Parents become *conditioned* to doing everything for their children and making all the decisions that affect them. And this becomes a difficult habit to break.

If you want to be a successful parent, however, you eventually need to give up some of the control you have over your children. As your children get older, they want and need to take more responsibility for their own lives. They want to make some decisions for themselves. They do not want everything done for them.

This is *not* an issue that suddenly pops up as children

enter their teens. Younger children also want to have greater responsibility, but they are less likely to fight back on this issue, perhaps because they still feel dependent on you. Adolescents, on the other hand, do not hesitate to fight back. They, too, feel dependent, but they also have a growing sense of their *independence*, of their strength and their power, and this gives them the wherewithal to stand up for themselves.

It is during adolescence that this issue becomes most visible and can cause the greatest conflicts. If, like the parents in the case study, you have controlled your children's behavior and have not let them participate in the management of their own lives, you are likely to have problems when they reach adolescence. Adolescents are quick to let you know that they do not want to be over-parented or over-protected.

There is another reason why parents may have trouble letting go of their control over their children. In the case study, Pam and Steve were *afraid* to let go. They were afraid that if they didn't control their daughter's behavior, she would get into serious trouble. This kind of fear, like the control issue, is not new. Nor is it something that just happens as children reach adolescence. Instead, it is a normal part of letting children of any age take meaningful steps toward their own independence. It's a normal part of letting them grow up. Think of the first time you let your child ride her bike by herself, for example, or the first time your child walked to school by himself. When you let a child do something by himself or herself—something new and untried—you are understandably going to be nervous or scared.

Although this fear is not new to you as a parent, it may seem different as your children become adolescents. The difference is only one of degree, though. Specifically, there are several factors that can increase your fear at this time. First, the penalties for making mistakes are greater in adolescence than in childhood. For instance, if your six-year-old experiments with sex with the neighbor's seven-year-old, the consequences are not likely to be very serious. But if your thirteen-year-old experiments with sex, one consequence could be pregnancy. Second, it is easier to supervise younger children than adolescents. If a younger child makes a mistake or falters, you can usually be there to help, but this is not always possible once he or she reaches adolescence. Adolescents' lives tend to be *separate* from yours. They tend to be out of the house and on their own, and this greatly decreases your opportunities for direct supervision.

Another issue that increases parental fear is lack of trust. In the case study, neither Pam nor Steve trusted Jessica's judgment. They both felt that she was immature, and they didn't trust her to make the right decisions. As a result, they became even more fearful that she would get into trouble and felt even more justified in controlling her behavior.

Parents who have this attitude find themselves in a vicious circle: By refusing to allow their children to take any responsibility for their own lives—in other words, by overmanaging their behavior—these adults hold their children back from becoming mature individuals. Realizing that their adolescents are immature, they further control their behavior—and make them even more immature. Further control just delays the inevitable, because sooner or later all teenagers are in the position of *having* to make independent decisions—unless, of course, their parents keep them at home for the rest of their lives.

What can you do if you have an adolescent who has never made important decisions and is, in effect, immature, but is now asking for control over his or her life?

The very worst thing you can do at this stage is to throw up your hands and say, "Okay, I give up. I can't do anything with you. You're on your own." By doing this, you are giving *all* control to your adolescent. But even normal, well-adjusted adolescents aren't ready to make all of their own decisions—and if they aren't ready, then neither are those who have never had any experience in this area. Adolescents will usually respond to an offer of total freedom by setting up situations in which they are, in effect, asking the adults around them to impose limits. Much of what is called "juvenile delinquency" or "juvenile acting out," for example—like running away and poor school performance—is nothing more than a non-verbal plea for limits. So throwing up your hands is hardly a solution. If you do this, the best you can hope for is to just survive until your teenager leaves home—and that's a pretty dismal prospect.

What *can* you do? Begin by doing what you neglected to do when your adolescent was much younger: Give him or her some choices within limits you set. Your job may be harder now because your teenager may demand everything all at once; it's wise to be prepared for this. If you're starving and you suddenly get food, you're likely to eat faster than is good for you. It's the same with a teenager and new-found freedom. Expect some arguments and some testing of the limits, but stick to your guns.

What if you have already given your children increasing amounts of responsibility over the years? Although your job is easier, much of what I have been saying also applies to you. Your adolescents will challenge you, too, and it will help if you set clear limits.

If you have trouble letting go of controlling your children's behavior, you may need to look inside yourself to find out why. One factor that makes the letting-go process difficult is the tendency to externalize your own conflicts onto your children. It may be that you have some unresolved conflicts about the control of your *own* behavior and are choosing to externalize this rather than deal with it. Several years ago I treated a rather successful business-man who was very hard on himself for not having gone as far in his field as he thought he should have. He attributed his lack of success to his inability to control his behavior at certain points in his life. Once, for instance, he had been critical of his boss and had been fired. Although he wasn't able to deal with this control issue in his own life, he did everything he could to make sure his son didn't make the same mistakes. The result was a fifteen-year-old who had almost no idea of what it meant to make an independent decision.

There are other possible reasons for the difficulty involved in letting go. Sometimes parents will over-control their children's behavior because they don't really want them to grow up; these parents still need babies. Other parents are afraid that if they do let go they will no longer be "needed." Whatever your problems may be, though, the only solution is to understand how you may be getting your own needs confused with those of your children and then try to work through these issues for yourself.

When I first began counseling, I worked almost exclusively with children and parents. A few years later, I found myself having to work with adolescents, and I didn't like this at all. I had had little experience with them and I simply didn't like them. (Secretly I felt threatened by teenagers, but I ignored this and simply decided that all adolescents were a pain.) At the time I didn't know why I felt so little affection for this age group, but later, with some help from my friends, I figured it out. I expected teenagers to react to me much as children did; after all, they were simply older children weren't they? But it didn't work that way. Teenagers didn't respond the same way children did. I had always enjoyed children's sense of play; in fact, it was the thing I most enjoyed about them. What I realized later is that teenagers *do* play—they just do it in different ways than children. For one thing, teenagers are much more verbal in their play than children are, and they do not as a rule like to get down on the floor and make monsters out of modeling clay. After I realized these things, I made a few adjustments in my expectations and got along with adolescents much better.

I also learned that many adolescents wear a mask. It's a kind of exterior "coolness" that seems to say, "Hey, everything's okay." This bothered me, because I knew that frequently everything *wasn't* okay. Again I was expecting teenagers to act like older versions of children. Children are usually straightforward when they talk about themselves, and this is something I really like about them. Having this expectation, I had trouble with the elusiveness many adolescents tend to have. But that was my problem and something I had to deal with. Nowadays when I talk with teenagers I try to stay as "loose" as I can—to "lighten up," as the kids today say. And my expectation today, if I have one, is that when I talk with teenagers almost anything can happen. And that's fun too.

XI. MANAGING GUILT

Almost all parents who walk into my office feel guilty about some aspect of their parenting. Sometimes it's only a vague feeling that they aren't doing a good job as parents. Sometimes the guilt is more clear-cut, as when a child has been physically or emotionally injured and the parents blame themselves for it. This kind of self-blaming can be very destructive—not only to the parents' well-being and peace of mind but also, ultimately, to the parent-child relationship.

Why do so many parents feel guilty, and what can they do to stop feeling this way? To begin with, guilt is no more and no less than self-blame. It's the feeling that you've done something wrong, *either in thought or in action*. You can feel just as guilty about having thought something as you can about having actually done (or not done) something. Implied in this definition is that there is something you *could* have done to make things turn out differently. And guilt almost always involves another person. That person can be living with you or far away from you or can even be dead.

Parents usually feel guilty about the things they have been *taught* to feel guilty about. This is an important point, because if you have been taught to feel guilty then you can *learn* how *not* to feel guilty. You may think it's "natural" for a parent to feel some guilt and that it's simply one of the burdens of parenthood. I'd like to suggest that while guilt *is* a burden, it is *not* natural or inevitable.

Guilt is learned and it is relative. If you think hard enough about the things that make you feel guilty, you should be able to trace them back to the way you were brought up, to your parents' beliefs and value system, to your social class, and to your ethnic class. While some parents may feel guilty about sending their children to school with dirty socks, other parents may not feel that clean socks are at all important. While some parents may feel extremely guilty if their children do not do well in school, others may not be overly concerned about this. If you have trouble accepting the idea that you are taught to feel guilty about certain things, think about children: children aren't *born* feeling guilty about anything.

When you feel guilty you are taking the position that *someone* is to blame and it must be you. But it's also very easy to pin the blame on someone else. It's almost as if you are saying, "The only possible answer to the present conflict is that someone has to be wrong—and it's either me or another person." This kind of attitude can actually *prevent* your coming up with a solution to the difficulties that brought on your guilt feelings in the first place. This is similar to the situation that arises in the family conflict; people in the family blame each other, and no one works toward a genuine resolution.

Society often adds to the burden of guilt that almost every parent carries. It's almost impossible to pick up a newspaper or turn on the television without hearing that the American family is in trouble. Why is the family in such bad shape? Perhaps the *honest* answer is that no one really knows, and it may be that whatever forces are at work undermining the family system are too large or too complex for us to understand. We may just have to wait until we can look back on this period before we can find any answers.

In the meantime, though, researchers and commentators on the family feel that they must lay the blame someplace. And they do. It's usually done rather subtly, because to come right out and point the finger of blame is not considered good reporting, but the implication is nevertheless there that someone or something is to blame.

Who or what tends to get blamed for the problems within the American family? Frequently, society itself is blamed. We are, it's said, going through a time of change which is adversely affecting the family. Does this mean by extension that we are *all* to blame? Perhaps, but it's hard to take this personally.

Sometimes our value systems are blamed, but that also means (if indeed it means anything) that we are all to blame. If the critics of the American family had stopped here I doubt if anyone would feel too guilty, but they didn't. They went on to single out the two factors they feel are most responsible for the decline of the American family: the schools, and parents themselves.

In response to this accusation, teachers and other school personnel do not, for the most part, accept the blame for the failure of the family. They are quick to point out that problems exist before kids ever enter the school system. Students are only in school six hours a day for eight months a year anyway, so what can teachers really accomplish? Besides, their job is to teach, not to parent! In other words, the schools side with the critics and point their finger at the only group remaining: parents.

If you are an average parent, you may say, "But I don't really *care* what the newspapers say about the decline of the family. I don't pay much attention to that kind of thing. So how can it affect me?" It almost certainly does affect you, though, unless you are one of those rare individuals who doesn't read *any* books or magazines or newspapers or watch *any* television. Even if you don't pay a great deal of conscious attention to the media, it's unlikely that you're not influenced by it at all.

It's bad enough that parents are blamed for the decline of the family system when, in reality, this is a social problem in which parents play only a small part. What's even worse is that while parents are singled out as being responsible, they are given no answers or solutions. This is a double whammy, and I think it's hard not to feel guilty about it if you're a parent.

The following case study presents an especially painful example of parental guilt and the harm it can do. The kind of incident described here—sexual abuse—is one of those things that can happen to a child that is very likely to make parents feel extremely guilty. Even so, this guilt can—and must—be managed in order for families to remain healthy. How do you manage this guilt?

IF ONLY...: A CASE STUDY

Heather was thirteen years old. She and her parents lived in a rather exclusive part of town, with broad sidewalks and well-lighted streets. Compared to other parts of the city, their neighborhood was a low-crime area and a relatively safe place to be. Still, Heather's parents worried about their daughter, especially when she was out at night. No place was completely safe, and Heather was a very attractive teenager.

Heather's best friend LeAnn lived about ten blocks away. Heather and her parents had had some arguments about whether it was really safe for Heather to walk home from LeAnn's alone after it was dark. Heather wanted to come and go as she pleased; she certainly did *not* want her parents driving her to and from LeAnn's every time she wanted to visit. That would be too embarrassing. With some misgivings, her parents agreed that Heather would be allowed to walk the ten blocks alone, although if she ever stayed past 9:30 P.M. she was to call them for a ride.

One evening at about 9:30 Heather called home. She was at LeAnn's and wanted to stay until 10:00 P.M. and then walk home. Her parents argued that 10:00 was too late. Heather countered that it was only half an hour later than usual. Anyway, she wanted to know, why were they all worrying? Nothing was going to happen! Reluctantly, her parents agreed to let her stay the extra half-hour and then walk home by herself.

But something *did* happen. When Heather was half-way home, a man grabbed her, dragged her into the bushes, and began tearing off her clothes. Only her screams, which frightened her assailant away, saved Heather from an almost certain rape.

When they heard about what had happened, Heather's parents went into a state of shock. The first thing they remembered thinking was *if only they had been firm about the 9:30 rule, if only they had stuck by their guns, this wouldn't have happened*. Over the next few days, they became increasingly obsessed with this idea. If only. . .if only. . .if only.

Heather's parents vowed that nothing like this would ever happen again. The only way to ensure this was not to let their daughter out of their sight. And they didn't. Over the next several weeks they took Heather everywhere, even to school in the morning. If she was visiting a friend, they called anxiously every couple of hours to make sure that she was all right.

At first Heather was glad of the attention her parents were paying to her. The assault had severely frightened her, and she wanted her parents' protection. But after several weeks she began to wonder if they really had to take her *everywhere*. She asked to be allowed to walk to school by herself. After all, it was light in the morning and there were people in the street. She could walk to school with her friends. But her parents wouldn't hear of it. They weren't going to make the same mistake twice. Heather was angry and argued that her parents were treating her like a baby. But they held firm.

COMMENTS ON THE CASE STUDY

You may feel that no parents would react like this and that Heather's parents were somehow atypical, but this is not the case. The abuse of a child, or even any serious accident, usually produces great guilt in the child's parents. This guilt often results in the kind of overreacting behavior evident in this case.

But the question is not whether or not you will feel

guilty, because it is normal to feel *some* guilt if something like this happens to your child. Instead, the real question is that of *how long you should hang on to your guilty feelings.* Some parents are still feeling guilty years after an incident—and I feel that that's far too long.

Can anything positive come out of hanging on to guilty feelings? I don't think so. You will simply be hurting yourself. Every day you allow yourself to feel guilty you are undermining any good feelings you have about yourself, because feeling guilty implies that you see yourself as having done something wrong. Eventually you will see yourself as a bad parent, and probably also as a bad person.

Still, couldn't it be said that Heather's parents *were* in some way responsible for what happened to their daughter? Wasn't 10:00 too late to let her walk home alone? And if they *were* responsible, wasn't it a natural and even healthy thing for them to hang on to their guilt?

My answer to the first question is that the parents were *not* responsible. It is very important for you to understand this. The one person who was *clearly* responsible for what happened to Heather was the man who molested her. *He* was the "reason" she was molested. He was ready and waiting to take advantage of *someone,* and Heather just happened to come along.

But weren't the parents at least *partly* to blame? Perhaps, although in this particular case that isn't clear. If Heather's parents had allowed her to walk home alone at 1:00 A.M., the ultimate responsibility for Heather's experience would still have rested with the man who molested her, although Heather's parents' decision would have been more open to question. But the real question here—the one that any parent who suffers from an incident like this will need to face—is this: What should be done about guilt feelings?

For you always have a choice. You can hang on to your guilt and make yourself and your family miserable, or you can make changes in your parenting if you feel that such changes need to be made. You can't do both—you can't hang on to your guilt *and* make changes at the same time.

The solution Heather's parents came up with was not a healthy one. Driven by their guilt, they ended up overprotecting her. But this solved nothing and in fact resulted in a strained relationship between Heather and her parents. In order to avoid future incidents like the one described here, Heather's parents may need to make some changes in the way they parent. But they will almost certainly not be able to make really constructive changes as long as they are experiencing such intense guilt.

I'M SORRY: A CASE STUDY

Marge was married by the time she was fifteen years old and had three children by the time she was twenty-one. She was a good mother and tried to be a good wife, although this was difficult since her husband was an alcoholic and physically abused both her and the children. Added to this was the grinding poverty the family never seemed able to escape.

After seven years of marriage and seven years of beatings, Marge had had enough. She divorced her husband and, with minimal help, set out to raise her family by herself.

The first two years were difficult. There was less money than there had been before, and Marge would sometimes not eat for two or three days just to ensure that her children would have enough food for themselves. It was a rocky and stressful time, and Marge could feel the anger and the frustration building up inside her. She tried not to take these feelings out on her children, but it was hard not to—especially with Danny. He was the oldest and, although he was still a child himself, she looked to him for help with the younger ones. But she found herself losing her temper with him more and more frequently. At first she only yelled, but then she took to cuffing him on the ears and finally to hitting him with a belt, just as her ex-husband had done. She tried to stop herself, but her anger and her frustration were too great, and it seemed as if she had to be angry at *someone* or she would lose her mind. And that someone was always Danny. Marge felt tremendous, overwhelming guilt for the way she was behaving toward her son.

And then things started getting better, at least financially. Marge found a better job and was able to make more money. She no longer had to starve herself to make sure that her children were fed. And, little by little, those darker days were forgotten. . .except for the guilt they had always made her feel. *That* she could not forget.

For several years Marge tried to make things up to Danny. She bent over backwards to please him, giving him extra privileges and favors. The other children resented Danny's special position, and this caused arguments. But Marge continued treating Danny like a king. As a result, he soon learned that he could get almost anything he wanted. All he needed to do was ask—and then that funny look would come over his mother's face and she would grant him whatever he wished.

But no matter how much she did for Danny, nothing eased Marge's guilty conscience. In fact, each new favor she granted only brought back the memory of those first two years when she had taken the belt to her son. She blamed herself, and she sometimes felt that she would never be a fit mother. She even wondered if Danny would be better off with foster parents.

COMMENTS ON THE CASE STUDY

I have worked with many families in which one or both parents have taken their anger and frustration out on their children. In some cases this resulted in outright physical abuse, while in others the abuse was emotional in nature.

Sometimes there was no actual abuse at all, except in the parents' fantasies. And, although this doesn't happen very often, guilt can result from *thoughts* as well as actions.

There is a major difference between this case study and the one involving Heather and her parents. In her family, Marge was the one who injured her child; in the other case, it was someone *else* who did the injuring. When parents injure their own children, it can be especially difficult to let go of the guilt for the simple reason that there is no one else to blame.

Regardless of this difference, parents who find themselves in Marge's position have the same choice as those who behave as Heather's parents did. They can stop feeling guilty, and make some parenting changes, or they can hang on to their guilt and feel bad. Marge chose to feel bad. In order for her to let go of her guilt, she would have had to realize and accept that there had been a period in her life when she had expressed her anger in inappropriate ways—*not* that she shouldn't have gotten angry at all, but that she should have expressed her anger in a way that didn't hurt another person. If *you* ever find yourself in Marge's position—if you feel angry and frustrated and tempted to take these feelings out on your children—it's very important to accept your feelings. Don't try to stuff them back inside yourself. Instead, take them as a sign that there's something in your life that you need to work on. And *do* get some help if you see that you can't deal with your feelings by yourself.

These two cases deal with rather serious issues, but there are less serious situations that also arouse guilt in parents. The guilt may be less inense, but it occurs nonetheless. A partial list of these less serious guilt-producing events includes poor school performance by the child; the breakup of the family; any acting-out behavior by children, but especially the use of drugs; destructive fantasies or wishes parents may have regarding their children; and the feeling on the part of the parents that they don't love all of their children equally.

****

There are two major guilt-producing myths that seem to cause the most problems for parents. One is the myth of the "perfect parent," and the other is the myth of "total togetherness." When parents believe in these myths they are much more likely to feel guilty about *any* aspect of their parenting, especially about any mistakes they might make.

The myth of the perfect parent says that as a parent you should have all the answers. Regardless of your circumstances and regardless of the way you yourself were raised, you are expected to raise normal, healthy children. This myth also means that you are expected to be a superb planner. It is as if you must be able to see into the future to prepare for *any* contingency. All this is supposed to happen because of some kind of parental instinct. Parents—especially mothers—are expected to instinctively know what to do at all times.

Of course, this is unrealistic and even ridiculous. No parent is perfect. No parent has all the answers. No parent is responsible for *everything* that happens to his or her children. If you expect to be perfect, then nothing you do as a parent will be good enough for you. You will be critical of yourself and you will almost certainly feel guilty.

The myth of togetherness says that it's always better to keep a marriage or family together than it is to break it apart, *no matter what.* Quite often the reason given for this is that the family should stay together because of the children. Even if the marriage is harmful and destructive for both partners, it's better for the parents to suffer through it than it is to break apart and have the children suffer.

As long as parents believe in the myth of togetherness at all costs, they will suffer intense guilt when they even *think* of breaking up their present family arrangement. And if they do go ahead and break their family apart, either through divorce or separation, they are likely to carry this guilt around with them for years.

In truth, however, it is often better *not* to continue a destructive relationship—better for the adults and for the children. Whether or not to break a family apart is always a very difficult decision to make, and separating is certainly a wrenching experience, but in the long run it is usually better for everyone.

XII. SURVIVAL SKILLS FOR PARENTS

Parents need some survival skills in order to take better care of themselves and make their own lives easier and their job of parenting less stressful. This is no secret—and it's nothing to be ashamed of. For example, every parent needs to get away from the children once in a while. It's more than important—it's essential.

IF HE DOESN'T SHUT UP. . . : A CASE STUDY

Ellen was an army wife. Her husband had a job that required the family to move frequently, so Ellen rarely had time to make close friends. She had always found it difficult to make friends anyway, and for all intents and purposes she finally gave up trying.

Ellen excused her lack of effort by saying that she just didn't have much time for friends. And her new baby *did* take up much of her time and energy. Her son Gordon was eighteen months old, and, although he had been a good baby at first, he had recently started to give Ellen nothing but problems. In particular, he seemed to be developing a terrible temper. Ellen didn't know how to deal with him when he threw one of his tantrums, which he did at least once daily. She was alone with him all day every day and sometimes, when her husband had work to do at the base, for most of the night. She was beginning to feel as if she was reaching the end of her rope. Whenever Gordon threw his food on the floor or started crying, Ellen didn't really try to deal with him. Instead, she put him in the bedroom, closed the door, and turned up the television in the hope that the noise would drown out his crying. But it didn't work, and she just resigned herself to listening to him.

One day, after a particularly frustrating morning, she

put him in the bedroom and slammed the door. Gordon immediately began crying louder than before, and Ellen felt that if he didn't shut up she would do something to shut him up. She didn't know what she would do, but she was afraid of how angry she was feeling and of the things she was thinking.

COMMENTS ON THE CASE STUDY

This is a tragic scene for two reasons: first, because it can be the first stage in a case of child abuse, and second, because this kind of situation can easily be prevented. Ellen needed to get away, to take a break in the continual confrontation between herself and her son. She also needed to develop some parenting skills.

Perhaps you have never been in quite this position, but if you have children you have probably felt often that you "just had to get away before...." Sometimes you don't need to get away physically, although this can be precisely what you need at other times. Sometimes it's enough to have someone to talk to. Whatever it is that you need, though, it's important to keep in mind that there *is* a way to get it.

If something like this happens when your spouse is at home, work out an arrangement whereby she or he takes care of the kids so you can have some time away. Unfortunately, these kinds of crises most often occur when a parent is alone. What can you do then?

If you have not already done so, make friends with other parents in your community and work out a plan whereby you can provide this service for one another. If you find yourself in the position Ellen was in, with no friends in the community, remember that there is almost always someone you can call. Most communities have a parental stress service or hotline with trained volunteers who will talk with you; some community counseling agencies and social service departments also have such services. In some areas short-term respite care is available, usually through social services or child protection agencies.

Sometimes parents feel too ashamed or embarrassed to ask for help. They feel that others will think that they are bad or negligent parents. On the contrary, the good parent, the caring parent, is the one who *knows* when to get help and then gets it.

Perhaps because they are embarrassed or otherwise reluctant to ask for help, many parents will wait until a crisis erupts before asking. Don't wait this long. It's much better to get away or to talk to someone *before* you feel like exploding or hurting your child. Spend some time with yourself and explore your feelings. Get in the habit of admitting to yourself that *now, right now,* you want some help and that it's okay to feel this way. Give yourself a pat on the back for wanting to do the right thing. As you think about this, look for patterns in your own behavior. Are there certain times of the day when you are most likely to need some assistance? Are there certain things your child does that are guaranteed to make you irritable or short-tempered?

Give yourself permission to have bad days every once in a while. It's not necessary to figure out *why* you are having a bad day, it's enough to realize that you are and would appreciate not having to cope with your children right then.

Many, many parents are in fact isolated, like Ellen, or they feel as if they are. Yet they are expected to deal with all aspects of parenting. The assumption is that you will have all the answers and that somehow you have learned to be a competent parent (although in reality no one ever taught you and, in fact, if you are a typical parent, what you know about how to be a parent is what you have managed to pick up from *your* parents).

What can you do if you find yourself having these feelings? Reading this book, or others like it, is one thing you can do. It's also important to talk with other parents. Share your frustrations, your fears, and the things you have learned that have made you a better parent.

I have worked with many parenting groups. In every group there are at least one or two parents who will exclaim, with much relief, that they never realized that other parents felt the same frustrations or had the same problems *they* did. Often this is one of the most important experiences they have in the group. It's a heavy burden to feel that you're alone, that no other parent has ever had to deal with the same problems you must deal with, and it's a great relief to realize that this isn't true. You're not the only parent in the world who has hated his or her children at times, hated being a parent at times, or felt like running away from home. Every parent has felt these things, so get together and talk about your experiences. Almost every community has a parenting class; sometimes these are offered through the schools or the community colleges. If your community does not have such a group, start one of your own.

Switching is another helpful technique. By this I mean that you and your partner should switch some aspect of parenting every once in a while. For instance, if your partner is having trouble disciplining your son, *you* take over. Or if you are having difficulty setting a limit on your child's behavior, let your partner take over. Switching can be done with any aspect of parenting that you find frustrating.

Switching is important because it helps to break up the "you-against-me" aspect of many parent-child confrontations. When arguments or disagreements have this you-against-me quality, you usually feel that you *have* to win; your ego is involved, it becomes a personal issue, and you become a less effective parent as a result.

Sometimes this you-against-me attitude occurs in those issues that you are having problems with in your own life. Learn when it's best to stop trying, when further trying will only bring more frustration; this is a sign of strength.

It's very important that you see yourself as a person who is separate from your family and that you develop this separate *you*. It is sometimes difficult, especially for women, to think of themselves as having identities apart from their family. But the most successful parents I have known have been successful people *first* and then successful parents.

Whenever I hear a parent say, "My children are everything to me. I don't know what I would do without them," I know that this family is either already having problems or will have them soon. What this parent is *really* saying is something like, "I am not important. All that is important is my children." This parent is also saying that all of his or her needs must be met by the children. These are feelings parents have when they have no outside life, no separate identity. These parents will have an enormous amount of difficulty in letting their children become independent because it is difficult, if not impossible, to let go of something if you feel that it is the only positive thing in your life. Such parents not only stifle their children's independence, they also stifle their own.

On the other hand, if you develop a life outside your family, you will be saying to yourself and others that you are an important person in your own right and *not* just a mother or a father. If you are able to develop this attitude, you will in essence be putting some distance between yourself and your family. Your first reaction might be that you don't *want* any distance between yourself and your family. You may want to be as close as possible. If you feel this way, you are equating distance with lack of love or lack of caring. But exactly the opposite is true, and you will find that you'll be able to give more love and more caring if you allow yourself this distance. The more you are able to see yourself as a competent person in your own right, the more you will be able to foster this same attitude in your children. You will also be much less tempted to see your children as extensions of yourself, because you will have your *own* extensions—past your parenting role and into the outside world.

How you develop your outside life or what you choose to do isn't really all that important. Just do something that is meaningful to you.

Much of this chapter probably concerns mothers more than fathers, because, although things are changing, mothers are still the ones who are most often responsible for the day-to-day care of the children. Whether or not fathers will begin to share equally in the care of the children is a real question. Although some fathers are moving in this direction, there are many social taboos against this. Men are not "supposed" to be caregivers. Men are not "supposed" to stay at home to take care of the children. If you are a father who has grown up with these role expectations, I urge you to take a closer look to see whether this is really what you want. And if you decide that you want to be more involved with the care of your children, then you, too, will benefit from the suggestions in this chapter. You will need to learn ways to cope with the daily frustrations such care entails. You will probably benefit from getting together with other parents, especially other fathers who are themselves considering making such changes. And you may need some help to see yourself differently. . .to accept the fact that you are more of a feeling person than you were brought up to believe and that caring for children is just as challenging and just as rewarding as any of the other jobs men are "supposed" to do.

EPILOGUE

Families are complex, almost as complex as the people who inhabit them. They need order and structure and consistency; they need rules and limits. But families also need to loosen up old ways of thinking and feeling. In fact, healthy families build a structure which allows family members to experiment and to be spontaneous. Maintaining a balance between this spontaneity and order is not always easy, but it will be easier if you are aware of family members both as individuals and as part of a unit and if you listen to one another and practice some of the techniques I've described in the chapters of this book.

The techniques within this book and the insights the case studies provide are useful for more than simply solving problems. Most of these techniques and insights can also be used after the major problems in your family have been worked out.

For instance, the family conference, while a helpful way to problem solve, also provides a place to share the joys and triumphs of family life and to learn new ways of relating to one another. What you will find as you gradually solve your more serious problems is that the family conference is deepening the positive ties between family members and is becoming a place of real sharing.

Likewise, the development of family members' self-worth is essential for the resolution of problems. But as your own self-worth and that of other family members increases, all aspects of your family life and your personal life will be enhanced.

Finally, I don't want you to believe that the suggestions in this book or any other book will enable you to solve all the problems in your family once and for all. That would not be realistic, for neither the perfect family nor the perfect parent exists. Even the healthiest family has its share of frustrations, tensions, and problems. I hope, however, that you'll accept this imperfection and that you'll work on your problems to fulfill your family's potential.